# CHINESE HOROSCOPES

We have known for a long time that we were influenced by the Moon. The Chinese have studied this influence since the beginning of Time: as our astrology is based on the Sun, so theirs is based on the Moon.

In this book, Western readers are introduced for the first time to this art. Here you are no longer Pisces or Scorpio, but Tiger or Snake, Rooster or Rat, according to the *year* – not the month – of your birth. The 60-year cycle of the Eastern calendar is divided into six series of ten years each . . . and there is a concurrent subdivision into dozens for the twelve 'animal signs' of the Asiatic zodiac.

So it's Leo the Lion here, Tiger over there: Aries the Ram here, the Goat over there – it's a game anyone can play. Which are you?

And who should you put next to whom at dinner? Who should be kept apart at all costs? Whose word can be trusted? Who loves to tease? Don't ask any more if people were born under a lucky star: ask were they born under a good or a bad Moon!

It's science fiction become science fact, in fact – the discovery of the Moon.

# CHINESE HOROSCOPES

PAULA DELSOL

Translated from the French by
Peter and Tanya Leslie

PAN BOOKS LTD
LONDON AND SYDNEY

First British edition published 1973 by
Pan Books Ltd, Cavaye Place, London SW10 9PG
© Mercure de France 1969
English translation © Pictorial Presentations Ltd 1973
2nd Printing 1975
ISBN 0 330 23424 2

Printed in Great Britain by
Richard Clay (The Chaucer Press) Ltd, Bungay, Suffolk

# CONTENTS

# LIST OF ILLUSTRATIONS

Drawings by Michel Brunet

# Were You Born Under a Good Moon?

## Were You Born Under a Good Moon?

Necromancers in the Asiatic countries, instead of relying on the Sun, as we do with our signs of the Zodiac, base their calculations on the Moon – or rather on lunar years. The question is: are you the child of a good Moon or a bad one?

The lunar year comprises twelve New Moons, with a thirteenth added every dozen years – which is why New Year in the East never falls on the same date.

As with our signs of the Zodiac, the cycle is a series of twelve – but twelve years instead of twelve months. The signs follow each other always in the same order. Each year of the cycle is represented by an animal, and this animal exercises an influence on the lives, destiny, and character of the human beings born that year.

There is of course a symbolic significance in the choice of animals: the rat is destined for the trap, the rooster has to scratch about with his beak and his claws to find his food, the goat bleats when there is not enough grass, the cat always falls on his feet, and so on. The actual choice (so the story goes) was made by Buddha, who had summoned all the beasts in creation before him one New Year, with the promise of a reward if they obeyed.

Only twelve animals turned up at this strange rendezvous, and to each of them Buddha offered a year which was to bear its name. They accepted, and the years ran, and still run, in the order in which the animals arrived: first the Rat, then the Buffalo, and then the Tiger, the Cat, the Dragon, the Snake, the Horse, the Goat, the Monkey, the Rooster, the Dog, and finally the Pig.

Nineteen-seventy was therefore the year of the Dog, 1971 the year of the Pig, 1972 the year of the Rat, and so on. And we can expect them to exercise their influence in several ways, for each animal affects not only the people born in its year but also the year itself . . .

So much for the legend.

It remains true in the East, nevertheless, that these signs bear an importance so crucial in the worlds of business, politics, and personal relationships, that nobody makes a move without consulting them. The year of the Fire Horse, for example (a special category occurring only once in sixty years), is reputed to be so bad for the family of a child born in it that many Asiatic women resorted to abortions in 1966 rather than bear an infant under its sign! This may seem extreme, but it must be remembered that the Moon has always been credited with an influence on human affairs – and there are certainly coincidences in this connexion that cannot be explained in scientific terms.

The man born under the sign of one of these twelve beasts will owe his strength or his weakness, his pride or his modesty, his aggressiveness or his passivity, his *naïveté* or his malice, to the influence of the animal controlling his life. There will of course be individual differences: from the moment of birth other influences, opposing factors, are warring with his destiny – the kind of life into which he is born, the financial status of his family, whether or not his parents were born under signs favourable to his advancement. But whether he is lapdog or hound, carthorse or racehorse, fireside tabby or alley cat, the broad sweep of his destiny will be the same and the main traits of his character will correspond.

It should be added that great differences can occur according to the season, the month, and the hour of birth, and according to whether it was a hot day or a cold one. Those born on the first day of their year will have its characteristics most marked and will have the greatest chance of success in life. This day, called the *Jour du Têt* in Vietnam, is the most important fête of the year, and people hang catherine wheels and firecrackers under their porches or among the branches of the biggest tree in the garden to chase away bad spirits from the house. Popular superstition has it that whatever happens to you on that day risks repeating itself throughout the year! It is recommended, therefore, not to work too hard, not to quarrel, to avoid creditors, and to keep out of the way of the Law!

This Asiatic New Year begins a little later than our own. It's a question of phases of the Moon, the cycle of years, 'extra' days to make the calendar come 'right', and so on. It would take too long to explain it here, but broadly speaking the year begins in January *or* February, and those born in these months may properly be either under the sign of the current Christian year or under that of the previous one. For the rest, there is no problem: the Christian year in which they were born is the one to determine their sign.

The information on which the calculations in this book are based came to the author through the courtesy of the Vietnam embassy in Paris in 1949. Through them, M. Hoang-Xuan-Han, a professor at the Lycée Albert Sarraut in Hanoi, was kind enough to furnish the relevant dates in our calendar of the various *Jours du Têt* since the Christian year 1900.

But the old traditions are dying. The Japanese embassy, replying with great civility to the author's questions, pointed out that the January New Moon no longer counted in the matter of making calendars, and that, to simplify matters, the Japanese New Year was now considered to fall on the Occidental January 1st . . . which leaves our Capricorns and Aquarius sneatly between two stools! So far as this book is concerned, we will give the exact dates of each Asiatic year affecting them as it comes up. And in the meantime, simplified according to the Japanese system, we can say that – given 1900 as the Year of the Rat – it is easy enough for anyone (except those born in January or February) to calculate his own sign.

It is to be hoped that the study of these Oriental signs will prove interesting, and that readers may amuse themselves 'conjugating' them with our own signs of the Zodiac – for a Tiger born under the Western sign of Leo is likely to be more of a handful than one born under Pisces, and so on.

All that remains now is to hope that you, the reader, were born 'under a good Moon' – though in truth each one of these Oriental signs can carry within it the seeds of success.

## The Signs and their Years

| The Rat | 1900 | 1936 | The Horse | 1906* | 1942 |
| | 1912 | 1948 | | 1918 | 1954 |
| | 1924 | 1960 | | 1930 | 1966* |
| | | | | | |
| The Buffalo | 1901 | 1937 | The Goat | 1907 | 1943 |
| | 1913 | 1949 | | 1919 | 1955 |
| | 1925 | 1961 | | 1931 | 1967 |
| | | | | | |
| The Tiger | 1902 | 1938 | The Monkey | 1908 | 1944 |
| | 1914 | 1950 | | 1920 | 1956 |
| | 1926 | 1962 | | 1932 | 1968 |
| | | | | | |
| The Cat | 1903 | 1939 | The Rooster | 1909 | 1945 |
| | 1915 | 1951 | | 1921 | 1957 |
| | 1927 | 1963 | | 1933 | 1969 |
| | | | | | |
| The Dragon | 1904 | 1940 | The Dog | 1910 | 1946 |
| | 1916 | 1952 | | 1922 | 1958 |
| | 1928 | 1964 | | 1934 | 1970 |
| | | | | | |
| The Snake | 1905 | 1941 | The Pig | 1911 | 1947 |
| | 1917 | 1953 | | 1923 | 1959 |
| | 1929 | 1965 | | 1935 | 1971 |

* The year of the Fire Horse

# THE RAT

# THE RAT – *playboy of the Eastern world*

| 1900 | January 31st to February 19th | 1901 |
| 1912 | February 18th to February 6th | 1913 |
| 1924 | February 5th to January 25th | 1925 |
| 1936 | January 24th to February 11th | 1937 |
| 1948 | February 10th to January 29th | 1949 |
| 1960 | January 28th to February 15th | 1961 |

The Rat is born under the sign of charm and aggression. At first sight, he seems to be calm, well balanced, gay – but watch out! Beneath this placid exterior there is hidden systematic aggression linked to constant restlessness. Stick around with the Rat for a little while, and you will soon find evidence of his anxiety, his nervousness, his quick temper.

The Rat is a creator of embarrassing situations, a niggler, sometimes a neurotic. He is always the first to grumble.

The Rat likes to be part of an in-group. He is a great party-goer and clubman, but because he enjoys gossip and scandal, he usually has more acquaintances than real friends. The fact that he himself never confides in anyone has something to do with this too: he is a self-contained man and he keeps his problems to himself.

Above all, though, the Rat is an opportunist. All

his life, he profits from everything around him: from
his parents, from his friends, from his relations,
from his own money as well as from that of others,
from his charm . . . Oh, that charm! He uses it and
abuses it without stopping to think.

Gambler and glutton, he does not know how to –
does not wish to – deny himself anything. Paradoxically, he is always frightened of failure and afraid
that he may lack the basic necessities; while living
intensely in the present, he dreams of saving to
assure security for his old age! The female Rat, for
the same reasons, stocks up her cupboards with un-
necessary provisions . . . which she proceeds to eat
right away! She's the one you see at the Sales, busy
buying things she doesn't need, in the hope of
finding a good bargain!

The Rat, imaginative in the extreme, is sometimes
a creator – but it is as a critic that he excels, and one
is well advised to listen to his advice. Carried to excess, this quality can become a defect and there are
certain Rats who go so far as to criticize to the point
of destruction, just for pleasure.

Sometimes mean, narrow-minded, and suburban
in outlook, the Rat is nevertheless honest. He has
the faculty of following through anything he undertakes to the bitter end – even if the undertaking is
doomed to failure! He can always make a success of
his life so long as he manages to master his perpetual
discontent and his insistence on living for the present.

Whatever he does, the Rat prefers to live by his
wits rather than by his work. He is happier making
a living by the sweat of other people's brows than
by the sweat of his own. Unfortunately, though, as

soon as the Rat earns money, he spends it. He denies himself nothing – and if he ever lends money, he'll want interest on it!

At the worst, he becomes a spiv, an engaging parasite, a moneylender perhaps, or a pawnbroker. A certain laziness, a fondness for the soft life, acts as a kind of cushion for some Rats. Perhaps this is why he makes a good businessman or politician. At the same time, the Rat is able to follow an artistic course with success. He is oriented more towards the intellectual than the manual.

Profiteer though he is, the Rat is nevertheless sentimental. He can be enormously generous to the person he loves – even though his love is not reciprocated. For it is in affairs of the heart that the Rat fulfils himself. The gambler Rat, the drinker Rat, the hell-raising Rat, the greedy Rat, is also the sentimental Rat.

From the point of view of romance, the Rat would be well advised to link up with someone born under the sign of the Dragon – someone who would bring to the partnership the Dragon's strength and equilibrium, but who would benefit from the Rat's critical faculty. The Buffalo, too, makes a good partner for the Rat. With the Buffalo the Rat finds a sense of security and feels the reassurance he needs.

The Monkey truly casts a spell over the Rat – even if the Rat isn't prepared to admit it. Mr Rat will fall hopelessly, madly, head over heels in love with Miss Monkey . . . and Miss Monkey will find that great fun!

The one sign the Rat must at all costs avoid is that of the Horse. Individualistic and independent, the

Horse will not tolerate the Rat's profiteer attitude. Above all, it is catastrophic for a Rat man to marry a Fire Horse woman. Fortunately the year of the Fire Horse (1906–1966–2026) occurs only once every sixty years, which limits the damage!

Rats should also be wary of those born under the sign of the Cat, for obvious reasons!

The Rat will have a happy childhood and a carefree youth. The second part of his life, however, may be stormy and troublesome. He may lose his money in a bad business deal, or his happiness in an unfortunate love affair. The third part of his life will be comfortable, and his old age as peaceful as he could wish.

For the Rat, however, everything varies according to whether he was born in the summer or the winter of his year. In summer the lofts and granaries are full . . . but in winter he will be obliged to go out and forage for his food, and he must watch out for the traps set along the route. In human terms, this could mean the risk of prison or an accidental death.

# THE BUFFALO

# THE BUFFALO – *for family, fatherland, and the old firm*

| 1901 | February 19th to February 8th | 1902 |
| 1913 | February 6th to January 26th | 1914 |
| 1925 | January 25th to February 13th | 1926 |
| 1937 | February 11th to January 31st | 1938 |
| 1949 | January 29th to February 17th | 1950 |
| 1961 | February 15th to February 5th | 1962 |

Quiet and patient, diffident and slow, precise and methodical, balanced and self-effacing, the Buffalo hides an original and intelligent nature behind a façade that is downright homely. He has the gift of inspiring confidences, which is the trump card of his success.

The Buffalo is a contemplative – which is probably why he likes to be alone so often. He can pursue an ideal to the point of fanaticism. He is often a chauvinist, sometimes a bigot – one of the reasons why he is often criticized.

Despite his appearance of tranquillity, however, the Buffalo is in fact swayed by a choleric – sometimes a violent – nature. Although he is usually self-contained and introspective, the Buffalo can in times of need command a formidable eloquence. Although rare, his rages are none the less frightening for that.

It is best not to try to cross him – for he can become dangerous. And notwithstanding his placid appearance he is a stubborn beast and hates to be thwarted in anything he undertakes. It's too bad for anyone who stands in his way: he can be very mean and he spares nobody. He is a leader of men and nothing can stop him . . .

He detests anything new-fangled: it upsets the even tenor of his way. You will find him, therefore, among those railing against Picasso, modern jazz, miniskirts, and long hair for men. He will never tolerate anything like that in *his* family . . .

The Buffalo is an authoritarian. His family, in the broad sense of the word, plays one of the most important roles in his existence. But his conventionality, his sense of the traditional, forbids any innovations. Females born under this sign can be relied on to cook dutiful pancakes on Shrove Tuesday and dress exactly in the way expected of them. It's no good whatever waiting for them to display any sense of sartorial imagination.

The Buffalo is a hard worker who can produce a great output and bring prosperity to those near to him. For the Vietnamese peasant, the possession of a buffalo is a sign of wealth – but the wealth benefits nobody but the owner's immediate family.

In the home, the Buffalo is a great guy to have around, providing he is doing his own thing. In business, he can succeed in the arts, or as the brains behind a garage, a contractor's, or an estate. As he is intelligent and good with his hands at the same time, he can make a good surgeon. But, above all, he is destined for agriculture.

He should avoid trade and public service, for his relations with other people are difficult. It is desirable, too, for him to keep off professions requiring him to travel, for this upsets his inner balance and his health.

The female Buffalo wants nothing better than to stay at home. She makes a perfect housewife and a splendid hostess. She's the one, more often than not, who wears the trousers.

Unhappily, the Buffalo finds all too often that those nearest to him fail to understand him. Although he is stubborn and dogmatic, he is deeply fond of his family and proud of his children. But he requires from them a total obedience and brings them up strictly: he's the boss and his word is law! In return, he is prepared to make any sacrifice for his family.

For the Buffalo, more's the pity, love is nothing more than an agreeable charade. He can be tender, devoted, sensual even – but he is never romantic. He distrusts the dalliance of lovers and is bored by the problems of passion. This materialistic attitude lies at the root of most of his disappointments in love and marriage.

People born under the sign of the Buffalo will never be jealous of their husbands or wives. But they will be jealous of their rights ... and the fidelity of a husband or a wife is one of their rights! For their own part, they will be sentimentally faithful – but they won't attach much importance to it.

The Buffalo's childhood and youth will generally be without incident. It is in the second part of his life that he will encounter difficulties, to do with his marriage. His partner may well take offence at his apparent indifference and seek consolation elsewhere in an attempt to find the romance so conspicuously absent at home. In such a case, if the Buffalo cannot put things right by the exercise of his intelligence, he will become so bloody-minded that he risks the ruin of his entire family. The worker, the family man, has no time for a deviation he is unable to understand. During the third part of his life, the Buffalo will suffer enormous difficulties, but if he can manage to smooth them out, his old age will be peaceful.

The Buffalo can make an ideal marriage or a perfect alliance with the Rooster – whom he will allow to shine undisturbed. The *rapport* between these two conservatives will be perfect!

All should go well with the Rat. Besotted by the Buffalo, the Rat will remain faithful until death. The Snake too, although frequently unfaithful, is wise enough to dissimulate its feelings and sentiments. In any case, the Snake will never forsake its family.

Like the Rat, the Buffalo is fascinated by the Monkey. To succeed in life, he needs the Monkey's genius for fantasy and imagination. But alas! – it will never work! The Buffalo and the Monkey will never settle down together.

Beware of the Goat, too, for different reasons. Capricious and fickle, the Goat can set the scene for a big drama because of her inconstancy.

Popular belief is adamant that the Buffalo should under no circumstances set up house with the Tiger. Such a partnership would inevitably end in strife – a battle that could terminate only with the departure or the disappearance of the Tiger: the Buffalo, the stronger of the two, would keep on charging until

the Tiger was destroyed. A Buffalo mother could
never, never get on with a Tiger child. Better for the
latter to leave home!

Finally, it should be said that a Buffalo born in
winter will be happier than a Buffalo born in
summer . . . if only because there is less work to do
in the rice-fields! The summer Buffalo, poor beast, is
fated to go on working doggedly throughout the
year.

# THE TIGER

*THE TIGER – the hothead in your tank!*

| 1902 | February 8th to January 29th | 1903 |
| 1914 | January 26th to February 14th | 1915 |
| 1926 | February 13th to February 2nd | 1927 |
| 1938 | January 31st to February 19th | 1939 |
| 1950 | February 17th to February 6th | 1951 |
| 1962 | February 5th to January 25th | 1963 |

The Tiger is a fault-finder and a rebel. He's a hot-head always revolting against authority and his superiors ... the stuff of which revolutionaries are made. He's the ringleader type – but unfortunately, as so often happens with leaders, he doesn't always merit the confidence placed in him! He's the one who's the first to cry 'Let's go!' – but in business, as in love and war, the prudent will think a little before following him. And sometimes they will be well ad-vised to hold him back.

For those who follow the Tiger may find them-selves heading for catastrophe. He's the all-time brinkman, and sometimes he pursues his taste for foolhardiness and risk to the limits of recklessness and irresponsibility.

It is difficult, all the same, to resist him, for he is a magnetic character and his natural air of authority confers a certain prestige on him. People automatically respect him – even those working against him. Which is just as well, for the Tiger likes being obeyed but hates himself to obey. Nobody dares to tell *him* where to get off!

But if ever he manages to think before he acts, if he can bring himself to listen to good advice, the Tiger can become an enormous success.

A fighter, violent and daring, he is capable of standing up for what he thinks is right – to the bitter end. He is obstinate and stubborn, contentious, and often mean, always quarrelling with someone. But although he is selfish in the little things, he is capable of great generosity, even of altruism, in the larger. Within his own terms, he is narrow-minded, and he trusts nobody.

The Tiger is always in the lead. He distrusts the status quo, he is against established authority, he is contemptuous of those who play it safe. Paradoxically, though, he can sometimes draw back when he is faced with an important decision and hesitate until it is too late.

Admirably suited to be an Army chief or a captain of industry, the Tiger will also make a redoubtable gangster, for he adores any profession that involves risks. Lady Tigers are the same in their way: they are always the first to launch a new idea, to take up arms against convention, to fight for what they believe is right.

Although the Tiger is not directly interested in money, it can happen that he makes a lot. He is above all the man of action, the man thrust by destiny into the limelight (nobody dreamed when Queen Elizabeth II was born in 1926, the year of the Tiger, that she would one day sit upon the Throne).

In fact this warrior is sensitive, emotional, and drawn towards introspection. He is capable of great love, but he becomes too intense about it and his affairs are rarely happy. The female Tiger will have numerous adventures – and all too often they will end badly.

The Tiger can spend his life with the honest Horse, with the Dragon – who brings to the partnership strength and prudence – or with the Dog, who will stick by him through thick and thin in defence of his ideals.

The Tiger should avoid the Snake, who is too wise for him, and the Monkey, who is too mischievous. In love, as in business, the bad faith of the Monkey, so skilful at fooling him, can do a lot of harm to the Tiger.

Buffaloes, too, are out. The Buffalo is stronger than the Tiger and will keep on attacking him until he is destroyed. If there is a Tiger and a Buffalo under the same roof, the Tiger will have to quit before he is annihilated (see The Buffalo, p 25).

As for the Cat, he never succeeds in making a home with the Tiger. The popular Eastern legend has it that the Cat, to annoy the Tiger, climbs higher up a tree than the heavier Tiger can manage – from which position he carries out his business (there is a franker word but I can hardly use it in a book that children may see!) on the Tiger's muzzle. But they understand themselves just the same, for they are after all of the same feline race.

The first phase of the Tiger's life will be smooth

and without any difficulties. The second will be violent and passionate. There will be problems of all kinds to solve – money troubles, family troubles, marriage troubles, troubles in romance, nothing will be spared him! And if these problems are not handled skilfully, there may be repercussions in the third stage – which can still bring him peace and tranquillity if in fact he does reach an old age!

The life of the Tiger can be completely different according to whether he was born by night or by day. Night Tigers, especially those born around midnight, will be sheltered from the snares of life a little and their path will be less hectic than that of Tigers born after dawn, and above all those around midday. It will be a stormy life, in any case, full of dangers – but the Tiger will never be bored: night Tiger or day Tiger, he is destined to bypass the easy life!

Not that he would have it any other way. Varied, thrilling, passionate, it's the life that he wants and the life that he gets. And his love of taking risks leads him to gamble with it time after time. The Tiger is the man of sudden and violent death . . .

But he is also the man of good luck: nobody enjoys luck like the Tiger. For the people of Asia, the sign of the Tiger is a good sign. It represents the greatest power on earth and it's an emblem of protection for human life. A Tiger in the house minimizes the three great risks – thieves, fire, and evil spirits.

If there are two Tigers in the house, though, one of them has got to go!

# THE CAT

## THE CAT – all for a quiet life

| 1903 | January 29th to February 16th | 1904 |
| 1915 | February 14th to February 3rd | 1916 |
| 1927 | February 2nd to January 23rd | 1928 |
| 1939 | February 19th to February 8th | 1940 |
| 1951 | February 6th to January 27th | 1952 |
| 1963 | January 25th to February 13th | 1964 |

This sign, symbolized by the Cat to the people of Vietnam, is represented by a Rabbit to the Japanese. But Cat or Rabbit, it is the animal that falls always on its feet. Cat people are the happiest, the people most certain to *be* happy; they are gifted, nice to be with, discreet, refined, reserved, ambitious but not too much so – and virtuous into the bargain. Nobody ignores them, for they are good company and know how to make the best of themselves.

But surely there must be a defect to go with such a deluge of good qualities?

There is, of course, and it is no less grave for being a minor one.

Those born under the sign of the Cat are superficial. And that means in its turn that the good qualities are superficial too.

The Cat loves company and company loves the

Cat. Cat people are great mixers and they adore social gatherings. The Cat is sometimes a gossip and a scandalmonger, but always with tact and discretion – which means in fact that he finds it difficult when there is something genuinely unpleasant that's got to be said.

Cats love to entertain and their homes are often beautiful for they have excellent taste. They are men of the world, sometimes snobs, perhaps, and the female Cat loves to show off her intellectuality and culture – usually newly acquired. They will study a subject in depth with the sole object of shining at it . . . and ignore at the same time other things that are far more important.

The Cat is not easily provoked. He is calm, placid, pacific. Sentimental rather than truly sensitive, he is more easily moved by personal problems than by the great wrongs of the world. Famine, warfare, and other global catastrophes leave him unmoved unless his own life is touched by them – and then he is so hard hit that he finds his position intolerable and allows himself to die.

This animal cries easily – but is as quickly consoled. The wistfulness and melancholy of the females born under this sign is one of the main weapons in their armoury of charm.

Cats are conservative, hating anything that disturbs their quiet life or poses problems for them to solve. More than anyone else, they need to keep their comfort and their security.

As the Cat is cautious – perhaps even a little timid – he will undertake nothing before he has weighed the pros and cons and examined the deal from every angle. As a result, people admire him and take him into their confidence.

Financially, this is a happy sign. The Cat is an astute businessman and nobody who signs a contract with him need think he can get out of it! In speculations he is fortunate and he has the gift of nosing out bargains. The placid Cat is in fact a formidable wheeler-dealer! He shines in trade, especially in some off-beat aspect of it like antiques, which permits him to capitalize on his good taste. Politics, diplomacy, the law all offer him equally good opportunities – provided always that he can live the tranquil life he craves within their orbit.

The females of this sign shine in all careers demanding taste, a social sense, and a flair for 'window-dressing'. A politician would be well advised to choose a wife born under the sign of the Cat: sophisticated yet discreet, she will make a marvellous hostess, add greatly to his lustre by being at his side – and revel in the limelight while she is there!

Affectionate and obliging though he is with those he loves, faithful and loving though he is, the Cat finds it easy to benefit his friends at the expense of those nearest to him: he's not really a family man, and that's the truth of it. Often enough, he regards his parents or his children almost as strangers to whom he prefers the cronies of his own choice. So far as female Cats are concerned, they can always be relied on to do their duty, but their maternal instinct in fact is strictly limited.

The Cat will settle down well with the Goat, whose artistic sense he appreciates. He'll look after the material side of the partnership himself and the Goat's caprices will not affect him.

The honest Dog and the scrupulous Pig will do equally well. But the Rooster will exasperate him with its bluster and its boasting . . . and as for the Rat – well, that has to be avoided like the plague!

Relations with the Tiger, in love as in business, will always be strained. The Cat, being of the same race and knowing all the Tiger's tricks, refuses to be impressed and gets himself out of the mess by the use of stratagems (see The Tiger, p 33).

During the three phases of his life, the Cat will manage to have the peaceful existence he wants on one condition: that he keeps away from the exceptional situation, the dramatic turn of events, the insurmountable obstacle. Wars, revolutions, natural catastrophes, are nothing to do with him: he wasn't designed for adversity. Anything that threatens his quiet life becomes insupportable: if he doesn't fight it, he'll go mad, kill himself, or abandon his principles rather than make himself a wreck.

The people of the Far East regard the Cat – or the Rabbit, as it may be – with a certain amount of distrust. Popular belief has it that witches and wizards change themselves into cats. And were they not burned alive in Europe in the Middle Ages under suspicion of trafficking with the Devil?

It seems, however, that this bad reputation is undeserved. Certainly the ancient Egyptians worshipped the Cat as if it were a god.

God, magician, or man, one thing is sure: there is usually something off-beat and mysterious in the

Cat's make-up, as though he held the secret to some great truth that he dare not reveal . . .

Finally, it must be remembered that the Cat's apparent weakness can easily be changed into strength.

# THE DRAGON

# THE DRAGON – *all is not gold that glitters!*

| 1904 | February 16th to February 4th | 1905 |
| 1916 | February 3rd to January 23rd | 1917 |
| 1928 | January 23rd to February 10th | 1929 |
| 1940 | February 8th to January 27th | 1941 |
| 1952 | January 27th to February 14th | 1953 |
| 1964 | February 13th to February 2nd | 1965 |

The Dragon is bursting with good health and vitality. Straight as a die, direct, he is incapable of meanness, hypocrisy, scandalmongering – and the most elementary form of tact or diplomacy! Although he is hardly an innocent like the Pig, he has the courage of his convictions and can easily be made to mistake a sow's ear for a silk purse!

The Dragon often gets himself into a state – for the worst of reasons. He is an idealist, a perfectionist. And his refusal to put up with anything but the best makes him ask too much of himself and of others. He demands a lot but he gives a lot too.

Irritable and stubborn, the Dragon is a real bigmouth and his words often outrun his thoughts: his heart runs away with his head. Nevertheless, however crudely expressed, his opinions are worth listening to and his advice is always good. People do in fact listen to him and his influence is considerable.

The Dragon is over-proud. He is enthusiastic to the point of impetuosity, and he loses his temper easily.

He is gifted, intelligent, tenacious, willing, and generous. He can do anything. And whatever he does do, he will do it well: as long as he lives, he will never be in need.

No matter whether the Dragon chooses an artistic career or a religious, military, medical, or political one, he's going to shine in it. He will be a success wherever he goes. He may devote himself to a great cause or a great work. Whichever it is, he'll see it through to the end. Unfortunately, though, this talent works two ways: he can be equally devoted to a bad cause – and equally successful in it. The Dragon just can't help winning.

He is often loved, but he himself loves rarely. He is never worried by amorous complications and never disappointed in love. It is he, on the contrary, who is frequently the cause of some drama of despair. The women of this sign are surrounded by admirers and often demanded in marriage.

Dragons are not prone to marry young; some of them in fact stay bachelors all their lives, for they are entirely self-sufficient and have the tastes of the solitary. To tell the truth, they are happier alone!

If he *is* settling down, the Dragon can make a good match with the Rat, for the warm-hearted Rat can take anything the Dragon hands out – even if it's indifference. But the Rat too will profit from the partnership and all the things the Dragon brings to it. For his part, the latter will benefit from the Rat's critical nature and taste for money.

Much the same sort of thing can be said for the Snake, whose sense of humour acts as a brake on the Dragon's pride. A Dragon man, moreover, will always be ensnared by the beauty of a Snake woman, of whom, as a mate, he will be inordinately proud.

The bragging, boastful Rooster gets on equally well with the Dragon. Picking up the crumbs of the Dragon's success, the Rooster grows fat on them himself.

The perfect 'other half' for the Dragon, however, is the Monkey . . . in business as well as in love. With the Monkey's guile and the Dragon's strength, each has need of the other – but only the Monkey knows this! It's worth remembering that, of all the signs, only those born under that of the Monkey can fool the Dragon!

A Dragon–Tiger relationship will hardly be a calm one. But above all the Dragon must keep away from the Dog – that pessimistic, anxious realist who won't believe in him.

The Dragon will suffer some minor difficulties during the first phase of his life, mainly because he will ask too much from those nearest to him. His parents in particular will be tried and found wanting. That artistic temperament will land him in trouble in the second phase: still superior to those around him, he will sometimes have the feeling of being misunderstood (though in fact he will be admired and his disappointments will be as small as his successes are large). The more difficult he is, the less is he satisfied. But he will be happy nevertheless – even if he only is aware of this happiness in the final phase of his life, which brings him everything he desires.

The Dragon is a sign of luck. It is the sign of the greatest celestial power, and is the most rewarding influence astrologically, symbolizing life and growth.

The sign of the Dragon brings the Four Benedictions of the East: wealth, virtue, harmony, and long life.

But every coin has its other side ... and if the Dragon seems at times to have more than his share of blessings, don't forget that the whole thing's a kind of trick in a way. The make-believe Dragon makes *you* believe in him!

Daily, he glitters and shines. But his lustre is all on the surface. He wouldn't really know how to dazzle, and his strength is only an illusion. The Dragon in fact is a made-up character, a fancy-dress beast, an animal for carnivals and parades, powerful-looking but placid. He can be made to spit fire, water, or even gold, as and when required. But when the party's over, we burn him – and then, like the Phoenix, he rises again from his own ashes as soon as the next one's due.

Can the rest of us really believe in him at all?

# THE SNAKE

# THE SNAKE – *the wise and beautiful one*

| 1905 | February 4th to January 25th | 1906 |
|------|------------------------------|------|
| 1917 | January 23rd to February 11th | 1918 |
| 1929 | February 10th to January 30th | 1930 |
| 1941 | January 27th to February 15th | 1942 |
| 1953 | February 14th to February 3rd | 1954 |
| 1965 | February 21st to January 21st | 1966 |

Snake or Serpent, he has a bad reputation in Christian countries – but in the East, on the contrary, he is well thought of, even venerated, for his wisdom, his sagacity, and his good-will.

So far as those born under his sign go, the Snake man is romantic and charming. He has a sense of humour. And the woman is usually beautiful, and successful because of it (Jacqueline Kennedy, Princess Grace of Monaco, and Queen Farah were all born under the sign of the Snake).

In Japan, those wishing to pay a woman a compliment and acknowledge her beauty are accustomed to say: 'My dear, you are a real snake!' – a pleasantry liable to be misinterpreted in the West!

The Snake dresses with a great deal of affectation and even a certain ostentation: men born under the sign always have a bit of the dandy about them, and

Serpent women rave, for example, over smart accessories.

The Snake never wastes time in idle gossip. He thinks often and deeply. He is an intellectual, a philosopher, a cerebral person. Yet he could in fact dispense with his acquired wisdom, for he has an intuition that is quite remarkable – an intuition that could become, if cultivated, something very like clairvoyance. Similarly, he relies often on first impressions, on his own feelings, on his sympathies, rather than on facts, on the advice and opinions of others, or on the experience of himself and his colleagues. He seems to have a kind of sixth sense in this way.

Determined to follow through anything he undertakes to the bitter end, the Snake detests being left as it were in mid-air, and he makes his decisions quickly and firmly. He will move heaven and earth to attain his goal and nothing will be allowed to stand in his way. As you might expect, he makes a very poor gambler.

He's a bit tight when it comes to lending money, though his sympathy for others often leads him to offer help. The help will be in kind rather than in cash, however: the Snake is freer with himself than he is with his money! The tragedy is, he *will* make it too much of a good thing, and his good nature always runs the risk of becoming intrusive. The fatal flaw in his character is in fact a tendency to exaggerate – in helping friends as with everything else. If he does somebody a favour, he becomes possessive towards them in an odd way, so that finally he is more of a hindrance than a help; his serpentine nature leads him to coil and cling to the point where he can suffocate the object of his attention. Think twice, then, before you accept an offer of help from a Snake: you could regret it!

In money matters, the Snake has good luck: he simply doesn't have to worry about it. He will always be able to lay his hand on money when he needs it, and he feels this so strongly that it's never bothered him at all. Once he has got it, though, he's a little stingy: that's why he never lends. What's his is his ... and in old age he can become quite miserly.

The Snake should stick to careers that won't involve him in any risk – even the risk of working too hard, for to tell the truth he's a bit lazy!

In love, if he does choose a partner, the Snake will be jealous and possessive – even if he no longer loves her. Those coils will twine and twine around her until she can no longer move. And this is often just to be difficult, for people born under this sign tend to be afflicted with 'the wandering eye', especially Snake men, who delight in different women. But both sexes tend to complicate their lives with extra-marital affaires. They would be well advised to struggle against this trait, and Snakes who succeed in channelling their affections inwards towards their own families gain enormously in the serenity and inner harmony of their lives. But that's where the shoe will pinch, of course!

The Snake will often have a large family – for him, it's just one more way of making sure that his wife has no time to play around like he does.

He will be happy with the Buffalo, who is content to be overrun by a family on condition that the

Buffalo is always accepted as boss – a role that the Snake willingly concedes in the home.

The battle between the Snake and the Rooster – if they are married or associated in business or friendship – will work towards the elimination of their mutual faults.

For the poor Pig, though, one can only have pity if he should fall into the clutches of a Snake. She will allow herself to be imposed upon, ensnared, immobilized – and the Snake will wallow in his faults, knowing that he can get away with it.

The Snake must have nothing to do with the Tiger, who will destroy him.

The first two phases of the Snake's life will be relatively calm. But watch out for the final phase! For it's then that his sentimental and passionate nature, and his taste for adventures, will play him tricks – even if there is the possibility of an undisturbed old age in him!

But everything depends on whether the Snake was born in summer or in winter, in hot weather or cold, during the day or during the night. He's best off in the heat, for he's frightened of squalls, of April showers, of the cold. The Snake born at midday in the heat of a tropical summer will be a happier Snake than the one born in the middle of an icy night in December. The destiny of those born under this sign is in fact so sensitive to the inclemencies of climate that a Snake born on a stormy day will be in danger for the whole of his life.

# THE HORSE

## THE HORSE – *a good man and true*

| | | |
|---|---|---|
| *1906** | January 25th to February 13th | 1907 |
| 1918 | February 11th to February 1st | 1919 |
| 1930 | January 30th to February 17th | 1931 |
| 1942 | February 15th to February 5th | 1943 |
| 1954 | February 3rd to January 24th | 1955 |
| *1966** | January 21st to February 9th | 1967 |

He always looks terrific, the Horse! He's got plenty of sex-appeal and he knows how to dress. He adores anything where there will be plenty of people – concerts, theatres, meetings, sporting occasions, parties, the lot! He himself is often a sportsman of some note. He knows how to make a compliment and to turn a pretty phrase; he is gay, sympathetic, amusing, gossipy, and always popular.

Above all, the Horse is cut out to be in politics, a career which could bring him great personal satisfaction with the opportunity to grind his own axe. He could be a winner here, for he has the facility to sway the crowd.

He is very quick-witted and he is right in there with you before you have had the chance to finish what you are saying: he's aware of the thought in your mind even before you've expressed it! This

* Year of the Fire Horse.

permits him to forestall any arguments – whether he approves or disapproves of them – that his opposite number can dream up.

In general, the Horse is gifted, as handy in practical matters as he is with his mind. But in truth he is really more cunning than intelligent – and he knows it. Which is why, despite that air of assurance, he lacks confidence in himself. At heart, he is weak ...

The Horse is hot-blooded, hot-headed, and impatient. Because of this, he is often apt to talk himself out of his ability to make himself popular. Those who have suffered one of his rages will never feel quite the same about him again. His fits of temper are inevitably a bit childish, and if he wants to succeed, he has to master them.

The Horse is selfish. He will trample on anyone blocking his way without the least remorse, for his ambition is all-consuming. He's a bit of an egoist, too, and it's rare for him to interest himself in any problems except his own – though he will on occasion intervene courageously in other people's affairs. Independent and self-willed, he will always go his own way – and he never takes advice! The sooner he leaves the bosom of the family to make his own life, the better it will be for him. He'll do it gladly, too, because the atmosphere of the home is important to him – so long as *he's* made it.

When in his turn he brings up his own family, he's going to be the hub about which the whole thing turns ... and he's going to love it. Everything will revolve about *him*: his job, his problems, his health, the ironing of his shirts, the crease in his trousers. (Though it should be said that this attitude is justified by the fact that his very presence protects the family: if ever he disappears or leaves them for any reason, the whole thing will come tumbling down like a house of cards.)

For if this egoist works only for himself and for his own success, his work nevertheless benefits every-body – and his output is invariably good!

The Horse is a worker, adept at handling money and a good financier. Unfortunately, as he's a creature of changing moods, he's liable to lose in-terest suddenly in things he's taken up, whether it's a love affair, a single deal in business, or a whole career. But never mind! – He'll start again with the same determination, and he'll enjoy an equal suc-cess. He can make it in any career that demands neither solitude nor meditation, for he is an extro-vert and he needs to be surrounded by people who approve of him and flatter him.

In his relations with the opposite sex, the Horse is weak. He'll give up everything for love. A Horse in love becomes besotted to the exclusion of everything else. That's why, in his life, he's so often left high and dry despite his positive gifts. But if he can manage to overcome this weakness, if his ambition gets the better of his passion, he can live happily and success-fully.

The Horse can make a good life with the Goat. Conspirators together, they can skate around the precipices of life while the changeable sense of humour of the Goat, the whims by which he is is seized, will bounce off the armour of selfishness worn by the Horse. Neither of them will be aware of it, what's more!

For opposite reasons, the Horse can live amicably with the Dog or the Tiger. These two, intent on the solution of their own psychological problem will pay no attention to the romantic instability of the Horse. So far as they are concerned, he can live his own life and get on with it.

Whatever happens, though, the Horse must not marry with the Rat – in particular if the Horse is female and born under the rare sign of the Fire Horse (1906, 1966, etc). Any liaison between these two passionate natures can only result in sparks which must lead to a conflagration.

The first part of the Horse's life, and the second, will be full of ups and downs. He will leave his home and family while he is still young, and this will bring its own disappointments. His love life will be by no means smooth. But the third phase will be a peaceful one.

The six decades spanning the gaps between the years of the Fire Horse mean that this rare sign occurs only in the years 1846, 1906, 1966, 2026, etc. These years are bad for Horses themselves and bad for families who have a Horse in the house. For his influence can change from beneficial to malign, and during them all such families will become subject to illness, accidents, and bad luck in general.

Men and women actually born in the year of the Fire Horse will have the same characteristics as the ordinary Horse – but they will be more accentuated, in the good qualities as well as in the bad. The Fire Horse will thus be a harder worker, a more cunning individual, more independent, more gifted . . . and, alas, far more selfish. His passionate nature and the frantic egotism which seizes him will lead him to commit his worst excesses when he is in love.

There are those who say that the Fire Horse can be a good influence in the heart of his own family. But popular belief asserts that he will make trouble in the home he was born in just as he does in the one he himself has built.

What we do know is that the Fire Horse will have a career that is more varied, more exceptional, more interesting, than that of the ordinary Horse. And that he carries within him the seeds of fame . . . or of notoriety.

# THE GOAT

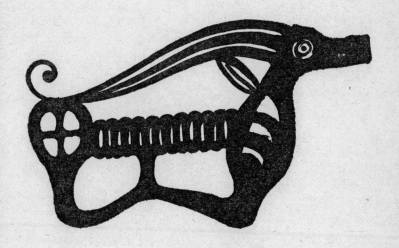

## THE GOAT – *the wayward artist*

| 1907 | February 13th to February 2nd | 1908 |
| 1919 | February 1st to February 20th | 1920 |
| 1931 | February 17th to February 6th | 1932 |
| 1943 | February 5th to January 25th | 1944 |
| 1955 | January 24th to February 12th | 1956 |
| 1967 | February 9th to January 29th | 1968 |

This is above all a 'feminine' sign. People born under it, elegant, charming, artistic, and fond of nature, could be the most delightful of all – if it wasn't for the fact that they are also pessimistic, hesitant, over-anxious worriers!

The Goat is never happy with his lot. The fields over the hill are always greener. Friends and colleagues become exasperated by his whims: he is a nuisance without knowing it. His lack of self-control and the mysterious delays which beset his life (he has no sense of time) make people lose patience with him easily, and though he can make himself agreeable when he wants to, more often he takes advantage of others – sometimes even living entirely at their expense.

On the other hand, the Goat sets no great store by independence and can adapt himself easily to any kind of life – so long as it brings him a minimum of security.

Shy, feminine, sometimes effeminate, the Goat is none the less ready to complain for he loves to be guided, to be advised, to be the centre of attraction, despite his eternal hesitations, evasions, and complaints. He never knows which way to turn, and always leaves the decision to others.

The Goat's manners are good and he has charm: it is only his nature that is so capricious. Those born under this sign are frequently religious – but whatever religion it is, it will only be practised to the point where it interferes with the Goat's comfort and everyday routine. He's not prepared to put himself out for it – though he is often drawn to the fantastic, the supernatural, occultism ... and the reading of horoscopes!

Men and women born under the sign of the Goat seem to be good-hearted: they are charitable and generous, and willingly share what they have with those less fortunate than themselves. Unfortunately what they share does not actually always belong to them ... It has to be admitted, in fact, that the Goat's sense of ownership is (shall we say?) elastic.

The Goat will allow himself to be tethered, but he pulls on the rope. Popular tradition in the East says that a Goat tethered in a lush meadow will stay calm and contented, but that a Goat staked out in one where the grasses are meagre and thin will never stop bleating and complaining. The observation holds good for humans born under this sign.

For the Goat, everything in life happens as though it was someone else's responsibility: it was circumstances, it was other people, or it was, in the final endeavour, good or bad luck. Whatever goes wrong, it was never the Goat's fault.

The Goat can be guilty of double dealing that disconcerts his friends. In general, he has no sense of responsibility, no initiative, and a weak will. He can make noises like a leader, but it fools nobody – for the truth is, the Goat was made to follow, to obey, and in the right circumstances, under the correct influences, can succeed thus in a spectacular fashion. This is especially true of artistic careers, in which, owing to his natural taste and talent, the Goat can do well or even excel.

The Goat will make a good craftsman or artisan and can confidently take up any career demanding a protagonist who is at the same time artist and technician, for there is plenty of intelligence there. But the Goat will never play the leading role – and it will be so much the better for him or for her. An efficient associate often makes a poor boss, and the Goat's whimsical spirit needs someone solid and realistic to lean on. For such a person, the Goat will do anything – provided a little flattery comes with the job, as it were, for the Goat also needs to be appreciated.

This, as we have said, is a feminine sign ... feminine because the traditions of the West have always assigned to the female the roles of dependence and passivity. But Goat men and women alike crave security above all else. The Goat woman dreams of marriage with a rich man, an affair with a generous boyfriend, or a liaison with some influential patron. Failing this, she will be happy living at home with wealthy parents. She is in fact of the stuff of which are made courtesans, prostitutes, ponces, management consultants, public relations officers, and other parasites!

She is also of the stuff of which great artists and great writers are made. Everything depends on the quality of the grass in her particular meadow, on the influences at work in her life, and on her luck . . .

People born under the sign of the Goat should at all costs avoid trade. They are terrible salesmen. They express themselves badly, their words are confused, they never know the right time to make a point, and they have a genius for getting off on the wrong foot.

Equally, anything to do with fighting or war is to be avoided. The Goat will never be a victor, never be a leader, never even be a soldier. If the worst comes to the worst, a Goat who has taken the wrong turning can end up on the scrapheap.

But thanks to others, the Goat will generally land on his feet. He will have no problems concerning what the Japanese call *I-Shoku-Ju* (the life of the senses, clothes, food, drink, and comfort generally), so great is his talent for knocking on the right door. If you have a nice country house full of good things and good conversation, frequented by artists, don't ever let a Goat through the door: you may never be able to get rid of him! For creature comforts are essential to his existence, the company of artists essential to the blossoming of his personality . . . and as for the country – the Goat is a real nature-lover.

In the life of the Goat, romantic problems will be frequent – though without importance – and emotionally agitated.

If the Goat settles down with a Cat, a Pig, or a

Horse, all will be well. Each of them can assure the Goat *I-Shoku-Ju* for different reasons. The Goat's caprices will be amusing to the Cat, they will be tolerated up to a certain point by the Pig, and they'll be water off a duck's back to the self-centred Horse.

No other sign can put up with the Goat for long, especially the Buffalo. If the Buffalo does bring comfort and security to his family, he asks a lot in return ... and the Goat has nothing to bring but itself!

As for the partnership of Goat and Dog, at work or in love, this is destined to fail. Two such pessimists, locked in life as though it was a pillory, will be eternally dissatisfied one with the other!

One thing is sure, however – whatever the sign of the partner, it will never be the Goat who wears the trousers!

The second phase of the Goat's life will be tempestuous romantically, but there will be a lot of luck in the other two.

And we must remember that, given the lush meadow, without any material worries, and well advised, the Goat can be a great success ...

# THE MONKEY

# THE MONKEY – *man with a load of mischief!*

| 1908 | February 2nd to January 22nd | 1909 |
| 1920 | February 20th to February 8th | 1921 |
| 1932 | February 6th to January 26th | 1933 |
| 1944 | January 25th to February 13th | 1945 |
| 1956 | February 12th to January 31st | 1957 |
| 1968 | January 29th to . . . ? | |

Of all the twelve signs in the cycle, this one produces people with the most extraordinary nature.

The Monkey is mischievous, high-spirited, a joker who is always full of fun – but he is devious with it. Although he's a sociable creature giving the impression that he gets on famously with everybody, this great *rapport* is often nothing but a ruse on the Monkey's part: he is in fact egotistical and selfish.

Playful, likeable, even obliging at times, he hides the poor opinion he has of others beneath this apparent friendliness. But, to tell the truth, he distrusts people from under any other sign, and considers himself in consequence to be superior to any of them.

The Monkey, it must be admitted, is vain.

He is also something of an intellectual. He has a great thirst for knowledge. He will have read everything, seen everything, briefed himself on a great variety of things . . . and he will be absolutely up to date on everything that's going on in the world. Cultured and well educated, he has such a fantastic memory that he can recall the tiniest details of everything he has seen, read, or heard. This is just as well, for otherwise he has an untidy mind and he relies on this memory a great deal.

Inventive and original in the extreme, the Monkey can solve the most difficult problems with astonishing speed. But once he has decided on a course of action, he must start right away; if he can't, he loses interest and abandons the idea without even trying it.

The Monkey has plenty of intelligence . . . and a fantastic ability to pull the wool over people's eyes! He is so artful that he can even fool the Dragon – who is strong, stubborn, and no fool himself – and resist the magnetism of the Tiger, whom he teases unmercifully.

The Monkey, as diplomatic as he is sly, will always manage to extricate himself from the most difficult situations. Independent and selfish, nobody's going to put anything over on *him*! He'll be the one who chooses, thank you very much!

He has few scruples. He won't hesitate to stoop to a lie or some piece of double dealing when it's necessary to further his cause. He will continue to be dishonest just so long as he is sure of getting away with it – for one of his characteristics is that he is very rarely caught out or found out. Certain Monkeys will stretch this elastic conscience of theirs to the point of stealing – and even if they are not all thieves, they are certainly all liars!

Whatever he does, though, he's so charming and

so clever at making himself liked that we cannot bring ourselves to be cross with him.

In a nutshell, the Monkey is an opportunist. And he's right to be one, because his luck will bring him every opportunity. Despite his negative aspects – the vanity, the lying, the unscrupulousness – people will always seek him out for his intelligence and the sharpness of his wit. Skilful in enterprises of great scope, shrewd and sly in money matters, the Monkey will prove an admirable associate and collaborator in anything requiring a quick wit, clear-sightedness . . . and perhaps a conscience that is fairly easy to satisfy!

He can succeed in any profession: politics, diplomacy, industry, trade – none of them will have any secrets from him. He can try anything. Anything will work – above all if he has been fortunate enough to have a higher education.

The Monkey has a good chance of becoming well known or famous, provided he is allowed to follow his chosen vocation. One thing only threatens his success: he must be careful not to open his mouth too wide. Even with his charm, he can still weary people by talking too much!

Despite a number of financial worries, the Monkey will in general enjoy good situations.

Romantically, though, he will not find happiness. Relations between the opposite sexes will be poor. With his exuberant character, the Monkey will fall easily in love – but he will as quickly tire of the object of his affections and look for another. Alas! He will never find a satisfactory one, for he is not a stable personality. Though he can be passionate, his critical sense and his clear-sightedness combine to cool off his ardour all too quickly. But his sense of humour saves him from disaster. Luckily for him, he knows more than anyone how to laugh at his own misfortunes and draw the necessary conclusions from them . . .

The Monkey makes a good partner for the Dragon, who can profit from his guile – while the Monkey in turn can make good use of the Dragon's strength. They can equally well go into business together (though the Monkey may always have the idea at the back of his mind that he might get the better of the deal).

The Monkey gets on well with the Rat too. The Rat, fascinated by the Monkey's surface brilliance, will put up with all his nonsense and love him passionately all his life – even if it's a one-sided affair.

The Monkey makes fun of the Tiger, but he would be better advised to treat him with respect. Any partnership between them, whether in business or for pleasure, is bound to result in fireworks. The Monkey cannot stand violence – but to laugh at a thing doesn't mean you can't fall a victim to it. The Monkey risks being devoured!

Whatever the sign of his marriage partner, the Monkey is likely to have a lot of children.

The first part of his life will be happy. The second will be upset and confused and his plans will often miscarry. The third will be calm – but he will suffer a solitary old age and die far from his family, perhaps accidentally . . .

# THE ROOSTER

# THE ROOSTER – *a show-off in the yard*

| | | |
|---|---|---|
| 1909 | January 22nd to February 10th | 1910 |
| 1921 | February 8th to January 28th | 1922 |
| 1933 | January 26th to February 14th | 1934 |
| 1945 | February 13th to February 2nd | 1946 |
| 1957 | January 31st to February 16th | 1958 |
| 1969 | . . .? | |

The people of Vietnam prefer to term this sign 'the Chicken' – which doesn't always meet with the approval of the boastful people born under it! That's why, along with the Japanese, we shall keep to the word Rooster, for this dreamer takes himself very seriously and he does like to be flattered . . .

The Rooster speaks his mind – he makes a virtue of it – to the point of aggressiveness. And this brutal attitude will not be without its casualties unless the offended victims overlook the rudeness deliberately on the grounds of 'frankness' or 'eccentricity'.

The victims who do this are wrong, though. Frank, the Rooster certainly is. He says what he thinks, as he thinks it, without beating about the bush – *Bang!* Just like that. But this frankness, far from being a desirable trait, is more than anything a kind of selfishness: the Rooster couldn't care less about other people or their feelings, and he doesn't

see why he should take any account of them at all.
Which means that there's one career barred to him
for a start: diplomacy!

As for his 'eccentricity', this is only an illusion.
Certainly he likes to be noticed, and he may dress a
little flashily with this in mind. But at heart he is
absolutely, completely, profoundly conservative – in
the political as well as in the general sense.

The Rooster is convinced that he is always right
and that he knows what he is doing. He confides in
nobody and relies on no one but himself. He is most
generous, on the other hand, with his own (unasked
for) advice!

The Rooster appears to be bold, adventurous, and
reckless. Don't believe a word of it! It's just that he
is full to bursting with absurd and grandiose ideas
that haven't a hope of being realized. He loves to
dream, to meditate, to build castles in the air, to
imagine himself a hero – but he is really an armchair
warrior: he dreams, meditates, builds, imagines in
the comfort of his home. He is an adventurer in car-
pet slippers, a short-sighted philosopher who isn't
really equipped to improvise at all!

Don't think that this means he's a coward, though,
or shy. In fact he really can be daring, given the
right circumstances ... and even brave when it's
absolutely necessary. He is sometimes a prey, due to
his dreams of being a hero, to the kind of foolhardy
courage that risks death with a smile on the lips. For
this reason alone, the Rooster can make a fine soldier.

People in general find him stimulating company,
but if he doesn't take care he risks unwittingly dis-
appointing them: being something of a boaster, he

always promises more than he can in fact achieve. Often brilliant, he is at his best in the crowded room and shines more in company than he does in the intimate situation.

Because he loves to dream, the Rooster risks falling at times into laziness – though his nature is to give everything to the job in hand once he starts it, and he has the reputation of being a hard worker. But he's for ever biting off more than he can chew, undertaking tasks that are beyond his strength . . . and if, after all his efforts, he still can't make it, nobody is more disappointed than he.

The Rooster is right to bustle about like this. Money isn't going to fall into his lap and he has to work for a living. But if he can control his dreaming and the cards are right, he can become rich. He has in fact the reputation of finding money in the most unlikely places, of drawing, as it were, blood from a stone. In Vietnam, they say that, thanks to the strength of his beak and claws, the Rooster can find a worm in a desert! – a simile that goes a long way to explain the continual and restless activity that characterizes him. But if by chance a Rooster allows himself to dream or idle away his time as he would like, he can easily become one of those picturesque tramps, the philosophers of the open road, that we see occasionally asleep on a bench or rooting about among the dustbins. After all, it's one way of making yourself noticed . . .

The Rooster is particularly suited to agriculture and to those professions which keep him constantly in touch with others, for he adores putting on a bit of a show.

In any case, with his extravagant nature, he's going to spend anything he makes as and when he gets it. He will be likely, too, to run great risks financially, advancing all too often to the brink of bankruptcy, ruin, and disaster because he has dreamed too much. This is no opener of a savings account; he simply doesn't know how to economize!

In love, he will often do himself harm to gain or to keep the affection of the loved one. He will disappoint her often, too, for the reality will never match up to the dreams he would so much like to share with her. There's one thing in his favour, though: he really is sincere about those dreams . . .

The Rooster man likes to be in the company of women, among whom he can show off, shine, swagger, and generally demonstrate what a clever fellow he is. But he stops at women: he very rarely goes out for a 'night with the boys'. Men bore him to extinction.

The Rooster woman likes the company of other women too (though that's not to say that men bore her!), and she chooses those professions which keep her constantly in touch with them.

The Rooster will be happy with the Buffalo, so family-minded and conservative. With the Snake, he can play philosophers. In love as in business, the Snake will bring to the partnership some much-needed wisdom . . . but he'd better be careful not to shine too brightly, or the Rooster might turn on him and destroy him!

With the Dragon, a Rooster will be perfectly satisfied to bask in reflected brilliance, especially in the case of female Roosters.

As a partner, the Cat is absolutely out! He won't put up for an instant with the boasting or the gaudy raiment. He doesn't trust the Rooster an inch.

The Rooster will touch the heights and the depths during the three phases of his life, business-wise as well as romantically. He will go from poverty to riches, from ideal love to the most sordid of emotional tangles. His old age will be happy, however.

Legend has it in the East that two Roosters under the same roof make life intolerable for everyone else. As 1969 was the Year of the Rooster, let us hope that those wives with one Cock already in the yard remembered about the Pill . . .

# THE DOG

## THE DOG – man of the Left in the right

| 1910 | February 10th to January 30th | 1911 |
| 1922 | January 28th to February 16th | 1923 |
| 1934 | February 14th to February 4th | 1935 |
| 1946 | February 2nd to January 22nd | 1947 |
| 1958 | February 16th to February 8th | 1959 |
| 1970 | . . .? | |

The Dog is a worrier. Always on the defensive, he never lets up for an instant . . . there he is, on guard, at the alert, watching.

The Dog is an introvert. He rarely shows his feelings, and when he does it's only because he thinks it's absolutely necessary. He's stubborn in the extreme and he knows what he wants. Frequently cynical, he is feared for his sharp tongue and his acid and disagreeable remarks.

The Dog is the original character who couldn't see the wood for the trees: he has a tendency to drown himself in details, to criticize things out of turn – and at every turn! He gives the impression of looking systematically for faults in everything he touches. This is because in reality he is the world's biggest pessimist and he expects nothing out of life.

He's always the first to speak out against injustice, often in circumstances requiring courage to do so.

He's perhaps a little blasé, but his critical spirit, his sense of ridicule, and his undeniable grandeur of soul save him from any accusation of small-mindedness.

At heart, the Dog is anti-social and he loathes crowds and all kinds of gatherings. Romantically, he gives the impression of being a cold fish (if you'll excuse the expression!) but this appearance is misleading: it's just that he's anxious and he doubts his own feelings as he does those of others. Despite all these faults, however, it is in the Dog that we find united all the noblest traits of human nature. Loyal, faithful, honest, he has the most profound sense of duty. You can count on him and he'll never let you down. He knows better than anyone how to keep a secret, for his discretion is complete. In fact, he detests confidences at any price, whether he's giving them or receiving them.

The Dog's conversation tends to be banal and sometimes he expresses himself badly. He rarely shines in company – but his intelligence is profound for all that, and nobody knows how to listen as he does . . .

As a character, the Dog inspires confidence in others – and the confidence is justified. He will always do his utmost for them, and his dedication can go to the point of sacrifice. People as a rule hold him in the highest esteem, and they're right, for he deserves it!

Throughout history, the champions of justice have always been born under the sign of the Dog. Every kind of injustice sickens the Dog, and he won't rest until he's done everything he possibly can to right it. (Brigitte Bardot, born in 1934, once ran a single-handed campaign to alleviate conditions for animals in slaughterhouses.) The Dog suffers for the sins of others. He suffers when there are wars, when there are disasters, when there are breakdowns of any kind, when there are unemployed; he suffers with the hungry of the world; he suffers for what's happened, for what's happening now, and for what may happen tomorrow. Luckily, it's not often that the Dog champions an unworthy cause – for thanks to his very doggedness (if you'll excuse us again!) he almost always gets what he wants.

Philosopher, moralist, man of the Left, the Dog couldn't care less about money. When he has it, he's generous with it and detached about it. It really doesn't interest him. Whether he's a lapdog or a stray, there's always a touch of the hippy about him, and it doesn't worry him at all to be without the material comforts. Even if he's in the money, his tastes are simple enough. (But if by any chance he should suddenly and urgently *need* money, nobody is better equipped than he is to get it!)

The loyal Dog makes a splendid captain of industry, an active trade union leader, a priest, an educator. But whatever his career, it will have in him a spokesman whose ideals will be profound and often original. He can handle men if necessary, too – and nations would do well to follow such champions, for under no other sign do we find united in the same person such uprightness, rectitude, and passion for work allied to so little personal ambition.

In love, too, the Dog is honest and straightforward. But he will have romantic problems all his life . . . it's his own fault, really: he provokes them himself by his emotional instability and his eternal anxiety. Like we said – he's a worrier.

The Dog can be happy with the Horse, who will let him get on with his Causes in exchange for a little independence. With the Tiger, life becomes a battle – the two of them against the rest of the world. United, they will adventure together in the name of truth and justice. The Dog in fact, in the nature of things, often finds himself teamed with the Tiger – and he'll play a very able second fiddle to the Tiger while remaining himself in the shade. But it is with the placid and serene Cat that the Dog has his biggest chance of finding peace and quiet if he wants it.

The Dragon is too proud to accept the Dog's caustic comments and critical approach. And as for the Goat – it's the Dog himself who won't tolerate people born under *that* sign! He's no time for her whims and he finds her selfish and superficial.

The three phases of the life of the Dog are all marred by uncertainty: anxious childhood, difficult youth; middle age defeatist before the amount of work to be done; old age full of regrets for not having done enough.

A Dog born in daytime will nevertheless be calmer and less anxious than one born during the night. It is after all at night that the dog's job is to guard the house – and thus he will be eternally on the look-out, always on the alert, barking all the time to scare away intruders and finding no time to rest.

For people born at night under this sign, it's a dog's life . . .

# THE PIG

# THE PIG – *good old Porky!*

| 1911 | January 30th to February 18th | 1912 |
| 1923 | February 16th to February 5th | 1924 |
| 1935 | February 4th to January 24th | 1936 |
| 1947 | January 22nd to February 10th | 1948 |
| 1959 | February 8th to January 28th | 1960 |
| 1971 | . . .? | |

Chivalrous (and that's the bitter end for a Pig, let's face it!), gallant, obliging, scrupulous to a fault, the Pig flourishes day and night the banner of correctitude and purity. Put your trust in him: he won't let you down and he'll never try to. He is naïve, innocent, confident, defenceless – a bit of a mug, in fact, if you want to be brutal about it.

To tell the truth, the Pig allows himself to be duped easily, accepts his own faults calmly, and those of others with tolerant understanding. Always the best of sports, he can never summon up a true competitive spirit himself. He's much too impartial to be sure that he's right himself, and he will keep on asking himself questions about the honesty (or loyalty) of what he can do and what he ought to do. He is incredibly sincere (to the point, sometimes, of doing himself harm) and the bad faith of others is always disarming him. He himself lies rarely – and then only to defend himself. Though he is intelligent he is a bit of a dunce about money, and as often as not he is downright clumsy in financial matters. Powerless against hypocrisy, he will often crucify himself in an attempt to justify his actions. He is an absolutely straight dealer and it's very rarely that he will accept a compromise.

Ironically he, who believes without question whatever anyone tells him, is always finding it necessary to produce proof of what he himself asserts!

The Pig's a splendid companion (often, strangely enough, sailing pretty near the wind, and game for a *risqué* evening!). He doesn't say much – but when he does decide to speak, suddenly the barriers are down and nothing can stop him until the subject's exhausted . . .

Like the Monkey, the Pig is intellectual – a character with a great thirst for knowledge. He reads a lot . . . but he reads anything that happens to be around. He appears to be well read, but in fact most of his knowledge is only superficial. If you were to test the depth of his understanding, you would soon find that it didn't go very deep. A Japanese proverb says that the Pig is 'wide of face but narrow in the back'.

He's a materialist for all that – a good-liver and often a sensualist.

Under his deceptive air of sweet reasonableness, the Pig hides plenty of will-power and authority.

Whatever his ambitions may be, whatever the tasks and the goals he has set himself, he will do his duty with all the strength he is capable of – and that same strength can be an inner force to be reckoned with, a force that nothing can oppose. Once a Pig has come to a decision, nothing can stop him carrying it out ... but before he arrives at it, he spends ages weighing the pros and cons – which sometimes gives the impression that he is indecisive and doesn't know what he wants. Nothing could be farther from the truth, but to make quite sure that he is avoiding any possible complications, he will sometimes ponder for so long that he destroys his own case.

Don't ever count on the apparent weakness of a Pig, though: it's just that he's a pacifist at heart!

The Pig has few friends, but those he does have he keeps all his life; for them, he is capable of the greatest sacrifices. He is extremely considerate of the chosen few who do merit his affection. The women of this sign like nothing better than to make presents for people and organize parties. They are marvellous hostesses.

The Pig's character, despite all this talk of impartiality, is a lively one and he would flare up often enough – if he didn't hate so much to quarrel (or even have a discussion!). As a rule, he prefers to give way in an argument, or pretend to change his views, rather than thrash it out. He won't even talk unless he likes you, and it's an honour if he condescends to argue!

One consequence of this is that the Pig, less than anybody, indulges in court cases. He's right too, because no matter how good his case is, his impulsiveness and honesty will always work against him to the advantage of those less scrupulous (we will leave to certain Asiatics the cynical reflection that, in order to win a court case, it is better to throw honesty, scrupulousness, and spontaneity out the window!).

The Pig can work in any walk of life, where his conscientiousness and aptitude for hard work will make him a success. Thanks to his basic sensitivity, he can do equally well in the arts – poetry, for example, or literature.

He can just as easily go to the dogs, however. One of his least sympathetic traits is that, once he does begin to take a turn for the worse, he'll end up wallowing in the mud and indulging in excesses of every kind.

From a material point of view, the Pig will always find, no matter what career he has chosen, that he's not short of the necessities of life. Work and money in sufficient quantities seem to gravitate towards him without his having to make any particular effort. People will help him all his life – and thanks to this help he will be able, if he wishes, to reach the highest spheres in the financial world.

Popular superstition says in the East that people help him thus – bringing him his daily bread, as it were – just to fatten him up so that he will make a better meal over the New Year! They say that because of this he is over-wary and trusts nobody. Be that as it may, people certainly tend to take advantage of his credulity . . .

Much the same may be said for his love life. He will often be deceived, often disappointed, often made a fool of . . . and often loved. The female Pig will make a good mother.

Pigs would be well advised to share their lives with those born under the sign of the Cat: for them, that's the surest way of avoiding discussion!

They must keep out of the clutches of the Snake. A Snake will make a complete slave out of a Pig in no time, enmeshing the Pig in his coils to the extent that the poor Pig loses all power of movement!

The Goat will take advantage of him.

The first phase of the Pig's life will be relatively calm. During the second, every conceivable conjugal problem will be visited on him. But whatever his troubles, the Pig, discreet and shy, will never ask anybody else for help; he'll try to get out of the mess by himself. In fact this reluctance to wear his heart on his sleeve may do him positive harm, for nobody will even suspect the hell he's going through . . .

If his birth-date is a long time before the traditional feasts, he will escape a lot of the disappointments in store for him – but the closer it is to the Asiatic New Year, the more he will be betrayed, ridiculed, duped, and perhaps, in the long run . . . eaten!

Perhaps that's the secret of the famous story of the three little pigs!

# Blue Moons and Red Moons

*Blue Moons and Red Moons*

We have taken the trouble to investigate the signs of a number of famous people, following our establishment of the various characteristics of each sign. The results, at times surprising and at times unexpected gave us food for thought. The fact remains that one must always take into account, when dealing with such men and women, the exceptional nature of their characters – which may sometimes underline the broader qualities associated with their particular sign, and at other times exaggerate the faults of the sign to the point where they become destructive.

## THE RAT

The first fact that emerged was the great number of famous writers born under this sign. Without even pausing to look them up, we can quote you some off the cuff: Shakespeare, Racine, George Sand, Tolstoy, Defoe, Jules Verne, Daudet, Katherine Mansfield, Charlotte Brontë, Antoine de St Exupéry, Eugene Ionesco. No other sign offers such a starstudded selection of men and women of letters (except possibly the Snake, but then those are all specialists in philosophy) – which must be encouraging for would-be writer Rats!

More surprising among these rodents is the presence of Mozart, Louis Armstrong, and Maurice Chevalier. We should have been happier, too, putting Charlotte Corday and Mata Hari among the Tigers – but they are Rats. And like Rats, they have fallen into the traps laid for them ... Lucrezia Borgia, on the other hand, was a Rat exemplifying the negative aspects of this sign.

Other Rats: Winston Churchill, Pablo Casals, the painter Toulouse-Lautrec, Himmler, Enoch Powell.

## THE BUFFALO

Buffalo people never belie their reputation for authority and sectarianism. So far as famous Buffalo are concerned, all we have to do is replace the word 'family' in our appreciation with the word 'nation'. Statesmen, war leaders, and dictators all find themselves under this sign that is at the same time authoritarian yet paternalist. They include Hitler, Zapata, Geronimo, Clemenceau, Vercingetorix, and Napoleon (whose brothers and sisters were aptly enough under the opportunist, profiteer signs of the Rat or the Goat!). Beside them, more on the side of the angels, Lafayette, Nehru, Louis XIII, and Richard the Lionheart.

Among the women of this sign, the Marquise de Pompadour seems to be a typical Buffalo. She had the reputation of being able to keep her house in order!

More surprising is the presence of Van Gogh, Jean Cocteau, Rubens – though to be sure there do exist

reasons for believing them in some respects to be
conservative . . .

Other Buffalo: Aristotle, Charlie Chaplin, Arch-
bishop Makarios, Dante, the painter Auguste Renoir,
Peter Sellers, Richard Burton, Johann Sebastian
Bach.


## THE TIGER

We can only bow down before the exceptional char-
acter of the men and women whose lives were ruled
by this sign. Among the latter we find Lola Montez,
Isadora Duncan, Emily Brontë, Marilyn Monroe
– all of them women who died young in dramatic
circumstances. Among the men are Robespierre,
Bayard (the 'gentil parfitt knight'), and St Francis
Xavier (there are a number of saints among the
Tigers; others among the Dogs, the Dragons, the
Pigs; few among Snakes, Cats, or Horses; none that
we know of among Buffaloes, Rats, Goats, or
Monkeys).

Beside those whose lives were accidentally or unexpectedly cut short, there are several great fighters –
Mahommed, Molotov, Ho Chi Minh, Louis XIV,
Karl Marx, Eisenhower, Bolivar, and De Gaulle –
and a few passionate natures including Beethoven.

Other Tigers: Marco Polo, Tiberius Caesar,
Charles Lindbergh, St Dominique, and Alec
Guinness.

## THE CAT

Cats get their big opportunity in politics: Fidel Castro (of whom one can hardly say that he cannot cope with unusual situations!), President Trujillo, Queen Victoria, Stalin, Catherine de Medici, President Bourguiba. They can also be philosophers of a kind, or theologians, such as Martin Luther or Confucius or Malcolm Muggeridge.

But can we say that Marie-Antoinette, Anne Boleyn, Eva Perón, or Garibaldi did a particularly good job of coping with exceptional circumstances? Certainly we can surmise that, born under another sign, they might well have enjoyed a destiny different and more advantageous than the one they drew ...

Other Cats: Pirandello, Einstein, Orson Welles, Toscanini, Field Marshal Slim, Arthur Miller, Stendhal, and the creator of Maigret, Georges Simenon.


## THE DRAGON

There is always something a little too bright, something of the conjuring trick, about our Dragon. The great actresses of the past – Bernhardt, Rachel, Mary Pickford – were Dragons. Beside them, grasping their success with both hands: Salvador Dali, Freud, Rostand, Edward Heath and Harold Wilson, Joan of Arc. And in all these cases, if you want to find it, you can see something a little larger than life, a little too loud, a little too exaggerated – something that makes us think of that carnival beast that we burn at the New Year ...

Among the Dragons, we are astonished to discover
... Jesus Christ! But maybe, as some people say, he
was actually born in 4 BC ...

Other Dragons: Jean-Jacques Rousseau, Barbara
Cartland, John Gielgud, Bernard Shaw, Danton,
Marshal Tito, Ste Bernadette, Napoleon III,
Marshal Pétain.

## THE SNAKE

It's among the Snakes that we find the savants, the
philosophers, the wise men, the thinkers – Darwin,
Montaigne, Copernicus, Calvin, Gandhi, Mao Tse-
tung, Arthur C. Clarke, Montesquieu – and the
idealists such as Kennedy, Louis Braille, Lincoln,
and Baden-Powell. Here, too, are beautiful women
like Mme de Montespan and Queen Astrid, and
writers of romances such as André Gide, Flaubert,
Edgar Allan Poe.

But you have to know their intimate as well as
their public lives to decide whether they are true
to their sign or not. One question certainly prompts
itself in respect of the above list: were Kennedy and
Queen Astrid born on a stormy day?

Other Snakes: Picasso, Schubert, Nasser, Baude-
laire, Brahms.

## THE HORSE

First of all the Fire Horse – and here the list includes
Cicero, Rembrandt, Corneille ... and Davy
Crockett!

Charlemagne, Roosevelt, Kruschev, Huxley,

Herzog – all of them workers, popular, full-blooded, egotistical – were born under the sign of the Horse. At their side, surprisingly: Pasteur.

It is said that the Horse will jeopardize his life for love. Mme de Brinvilliers poisoned for love. Edward VIII abdicated ...

Other Horses: Delacroix, Newton, Georges Braque, Buffalo Bill, King Baudouin.

## THE GOAT

Plenty of actors and artists among the capricious, temperamental Goats: Douglas Fairbanks, Sir Malcolm Sargent, Rudolph Valentino, Tino Rossi, Françoise Arnoul, Laurence Olivier ... and then Michelangelo succeeded thanks to his patrons, and Balzac very often through the generosity of his mother. Diane de Poitiers became a courtesan ...

We find under this sign too (a little more subtly): John Ford, Mussolini, Claudette Colbert, Cesare Borgia.

Other Goats: Théophile Gautier, Cervantes, the film director H. G. Clouzot.

## THE MONKEY

We have to admit that the majority of men in politics were born under the sign of the Monkey. For instance: Lyndon Johnson, Poincaré, Daladier, Truman, Julius Caesar, Chamberlain.

Under the same sign we find three painters – Leonardo da Vinci, Modigliani, Gauguin – and several poets or writers – Milton, Byron, Dickens and Alexandre Dumas.

We also find the Marquis de Sade . . .

Did they all have a fantastic memory, incredible charm, and a conscience that was 'elastic'? Maybe . . . but what we can say is that most of them did in fact die solitary deaths.

Other Monkeys: Buster Keaton, Captain Cook, Michèle Morgan, Elizabeth Taylor, the great documentary film-maker Robert Flaherty.


## THE ROOSTER

Roosters, it is well known, like to strut about and wear uniform – and so we are not surprised to find under this sign Richelieu, Goebbels, Kléber, and Raymond Oliver. Other characteristics of the Rooster are exemplified in Maria de Medici and Paul VI.

Other Roosters: François Mauriac, André Maurois, William Faulkner, Wagner, Descartes, Kipling, La Fontaine, the authoress Colette, and Clyde (of Bonnie and Clyde, perhaps the most typical of all).


## THE DOG

It's under this sign that we find all the champions of justice, as we might expect. Here are Bertolt Brecht, Lenin, Voltaire, Socrates, Molière, Léon Blum . . .

What else can we say? Anxiety, cynicism, lucidity, detachment, acid comments – they are all there in one guise or another. It's true that the presence of

Rasputin among the Dogs is a surprise – but what do we know of a man's inner character . . . ?

Other Dogs: Proust, Yuri Gagarin, Feydeau, de Maupassant, Louis XVI.

## THE PIG

As for the good old Pig, he doesn't belie his reputation of never being in need: the first Rothschild, the first Rockefeller, and the first Ford were all Pigs! So, for that matter, was St Ignatius Loyola, the founder of the Jesuits . . .

By their sides we find Federico Garcia Lorca, François Villon, Dr Albert Schweitzer – all of them men of good-will, all of them to some extent dupes or scapegoats, all of them in a way losers. We find firm and authoritarian men like Pascal, Le Corbusier, Field-Marshal Montgomery, Marshal Foch, and Georges Pompidou; we find those like Henry VIII and Bismarck, who roll about in the mud to besmirch themselves. None of them were ever in need . . .

Other Pigs: Oliver Cromwell, Mme de Maintenon, Françoise Sagan.

We leave you the result of this small piece of research in the hope that it will make you think – and that it will inspire you to look up the birthdates of your own idols, your friends and relations, and those famous men and women whom you most admire.

Try to find out more about the examples we have given in the previous pages. Think, too, of their month of birth – for even in the Eastern horoscope the sun has his say. And you can cross-check with our own Zodiacal signs through the chart at the end of the book.

Enjoy yourself, anyway! The Sun has a date with the Moon!

## Conclusion

These Asiatic horoscopes are as old as our own and enjoy the same reputation in the countries of the East as those based on the monthly signs of the Zodiac do in the West.

For centuries, seven hundred millions of Chinese built their lives around the forecasts of their particular horoscope, especially those given in the so-called Imperial Almanac. In this publication, each year specialized and detailed predictions forecast the future for each sign and for the year as a whole. Alongside these were long-range meteorological forecasts, formulae for conciliating the spirits, lists of forbidden things to do in that year, and recipes for medicine, magic, and . . . the kitchen!

It was in any case well known that certain signs were absolutely incompatible one with another, and the 'forbidden things' lists were explicit in their refusal to tolerate the marriage of a Tiger with a Buffalo, a Horse with a Rat, and so on.

Such beliefs would have repercussions on family life, on friendships, on business, and in politics. Who knows what broken romances, what ruined business deals, what political careers compromised were the result of consulting these horoscopes!

But what is their position in present-day China, the land of the Five-Year Plan and the Red Guard? Mao has forbidden them; the fact that he was

born under the sign of the Snake leaves us wonder-
ing . . .

But since we are not Chinese, there is nothing to
stop us amusing ourselves with this age-old game
which has, it seems, a great deal of truth in it.

Don't do any business, don't begin any friendships
or adventures, without consulting these tables and
charts – but don't take it too seriously either: it is
only a game, and it's not going to affect your destiny!

But if you attach an equal importance to the signs
of the Zodiac, as we have already said, there is nothing to stop you 'conjugating' the two horoscopes
and making a cross-reference between them.

Perhaps you will, between the two of them,
recognize yourself!

# Appendices

# THE VIETNAMESE CALENDAR

The year 1970 is the 4607th year of the lunar calendar adopted in 2637 BC by the Sino-Vietnamese races. This calendar is calculated in sixty-year cycles and is now in its 77th cycle – which started in 1924 and will end in 1984. Every year of 355 days is placed under the sign of one of the twelve animals of the oriental 'zodiac'. At the same time, each cycle is further subdivided into six series of ten years each.

Take, for example, the Christian year 1900, the first in the tables over the page. The day in our calendar corresponding to the New Year *Jour du Têt* in the cyclic calendar – last column: Cauh-Ti': 7th Rat in the cycle of 60, divided into six series of 10, ie, No 37 in the cycle – is January 31st.

The central column marked with an 'm' indicates if the relevant cyclic year is with or without an intercalary month. Where this is so marked, the number in the column refers to the month affected.

| Christian year | | | | Vietnamese year | |
|---|---|---|---|---|---|
| Year | Day | Month | M | Sign | No |
| 1900 | 31 | 1 | 8th | 7th Rat | 37 |
| 01 | 19 | 2 | | 8th Buffalo | 38 |
| 02 | 8 | 2 | | 9th Tiger | 39 |
| 03 | 29 | 1 | 5th | 10th Cat | 40 |
| 04 | 16 | 2 | | 1st Dragon | 41 |

| Christian year | | | | Vietnamese year | |
|---|---|---|---|---|---|
| Year | Day | Month | M | Sign | No |
| 05 | 4 | 2 | | 2nd Snake | 42 |
| 06 | 25 | 1 | 4th | 3rd Horse | 43 |
| 07 | 13 | 2 | | 4th Goat | 44 |
| 08 | 2 | 2 | | 5th Monkey | 45 |
| 09 | 22 | 1 | 2nd | 6th Rooster | 46 |
| 1910 | 10 | 2 | | 7th Dog | 47 |
| 11 | 30 | 1 | 6th | 8th Pig | 48 |
| 12 | 18 | 2 | | 9th Rat | 49 |
| 13 | 6 | 2 | | 10th Buffalo | 50 |
| 14 | 26 | 1 | 5th | 1st Tiger | 51 |
| 15 | 14 | 2 | | 2nd Cat | 52 |
| 16 | 3 | 2 | | 3rd Dragon | 53 |
| 17 | 23 | 1 | 2nd | 4th Snake | 54 |
| 18 | 11 | 2 | | 5th Horse | 55 |
| 19 | 1 | 2 | 7th | 6th Goat | 56 |
| 1920 | 20 | 2 | | 7th Monkey | 57 |
| 21 | 8 | 2 | | 8th Rooster | 58 |
| 22 | 28 | 1 | 5th | 9th Dog | 59 |
| 23 | 16 | 2 | | 10th Pig | 60 |
| 24 | 5 | 2 | | 1st Rat | 1 |
| 25 | 25 | 1 | 4th | 2nd Buffalo | 2 |
| 26 | 13 | 2 | | 3rd Tiger | 3 |
| 27 | 2 | 2 | | 4th Cat | 4 |
| 28 | 23 | 1 | 2nd | 5th Dragon | 5 |
| 29 | 10 | 2 | | 6th Snake | 6 |
| 1930 | 30 | 1 | 6th | 7th Horse | 7 |
| 31 | 17 | 2 | | 8th Goat | 8 |
| 32 | 6 | 2 | | 9th Monkey | 9 |
| 33 | 26 | 1 | 5th | 10th Rooster | 10 |
| 34 | 14 | 2 | | 1st Dog | 11 |

| Christian year | | | | Vietnamese year | |
|---|---|---|---|---|---|
| Year | Day | Month | M | Sign | No |
| 35 | 4 | 2 | | 2nd Pig | 12 |
| 36 | 24 | 1 | 3rd | 3rd Rat | 13 |
| 37 | 11 | 2 | | 4th Buffalo | 14 |
| 38 | 31 | 1 | 7th | 5th Tiger | 15 |
| 39 | 19 | 2 | | 6th Cat | 16 |
| 1940 | 8 | 2 | | 7th Dragon | 17 |
| 41 | 27 | 1 | 6th | 8th Snake | 18 |
| 42 | 15 | 2 | | 9th Horse | 19 |
| 43 | 5 | 2 | | 10th Goat | 20 |
| 44 | 25 | 1 | 4th | 1st Monkey | 21 |
| 45 | 13 | 2 | | 2nd Rooster | 22 |
| 46 | 2 | 2 | | 3rd Dog | 23 |
| 47 | 22 | 1 | 2nd | 4th Pig | 24 |
| 48 | 10 | 2 | | 5th Rat | 25 |
| 49 | 29 | 1 | 7th | 6th Buffalo | 26 |
| 1950 | 17 | 2 | | 7th Tiger | 27 |

# The Years and Their Signs

## THE YEAR OF THE RAT

1948   1960   1972   1984   etc

*Make economies to save up for lean years to come. A year favourable for jams and preserves, for purchases, loans, and investments. Apparently a good year financially, it may merely hide the miseries of the future.*

*Politically, there will be surprises, accusations, condemnations.*

*A good year for literature. Children born in the year of the Rat will be happier if born in summer.*

*THE RAT* – Rats will be protected this year. Happy in business and in love. If he should write a novel, the Rat should make sure it is submitted to a publisher before the end of the year!

*THE BUFFALO* – Should take advantage of the general trend of the year to put aside money for a rainy day. A good year for Buffalo from all points of view.

*THE TIGER* – Best thing for Tigers to do is take a look into the future – for there is nothing for them in this year: so far as they are concerned, it's a dead loss!

*THE CAT* – Be careful in business and don't put too much trust in friends. This could be a year of betrayals . . .

*THE DRAGON* – A good year! Take advantage of it by making investments. And hope for a romance with a Rat . . .

*THE SNAKE* – A bit too hectic for the Snake, this year – but there's not much he couldn't do. He's so damned clever!

*THE HORSE* – A bad year. The Rat will do his best to harm him. In business as in love – take care!

*THE GOAT* – Better to stay in the country away from it all and count on the economies of others for the Goat won't know how to do it herself.

*THE MONKEY* – An excellent year for Monkeys. Everything they touch will be a success . . . and if by chance a Rat should fall in love with one, you'll see the happiest Monkey on earth!

*THE ROOSTER* – Watch out for bad business deals! There's a tendency for Roosters (dare we say it?) to put all their eggs in one basket . . .

*THE DOG* – Investments won't interest him unless they pay bigger dividends than they do here. He will be bored.

*THE PIG* – Pigs will do very good business this year. They could find real love. A vintage year for them.

# THE YEAR OF THE BUFFALO

## 1949   1961   1973   1985   etc

*Too much work for everyone, this year . . . we
risk working ourselves to death! Cultivate your
garden, buy a farm, improve the farm you
already have.*

*Conservatives carry off the political prizes. Risk
of dictatorship.*

*In general, a year favourable to agriculture: the
farmer can sleep in peace, for there will be no
drought, no hailstorms, no excess rainfall, no in-
vasion of locusts! Buffalo born in winter will have
less of a job to make a living . . . so let's hope the
baby will come between November and March.*

*THE RAT* – Just as well for Master and Mistress Rat
that they made those economies last year: they're
not too fond of hard work!

*THE BUFFALO* – An excellent year, of course.
Hard work will pay dividends – and conscientious
Buffalo will be rewarded by authority. Those not
yet married would do well to consider starting a
family.

*THE TIGER* – The worst year of all for Tigers.
Start nothing new. Take no risks.

*THE CAT* – One way and another – providing plenty
of tact and diplomacy are in evidence – the Cat

should just about make it without coming to any harm!

*THE DRAGON* – Dragons don't take kindly to people who throw their weight about. Happily they are strong enough themselves to stand out against them.

*THE SNAKE* – Too much hard work about here! The Snake is too lazy for the year of the Buffalo. Better wait quietly until it's all over . . .

*THE HORSE* – Excellent from a business point of view, this year may turn out to be a disappointment romantically.

*THE GOAT* – Terrible year for the poor Goat! One can, after all, be fond of the country without being mad about farming!

*THE MONKEY* – All is well! Those who act as go-betweens will get by. The Buffalo will make use of Monkeys as men (or maids) of all work . . .

*THE ROOSTER* – A splendid year. Happy, triumphant, laughing behind his hand (or claw), the Rooster will be in his element . . . and what if he does have to work? He knows how to do it!

*THE DOG* – A disastrous year. If there are revolutions to be plotted, this is the year in which Dogs will plan them – and take too many risks . . .

*THE PIG* – Even if it's in a critical spirit, the Pig will adapt himself to the prevailing conditions. Better not run the risk of making him lose his temper, though.

# THE YEAR OF THE TIGER

## 1950   1962   1974   1986   etc

*This will not be an entirely peaceful year. Expect changes in life – but be careful.*

*Politically, there will be major realignments . . . theatrical coups . . . revolution . . . prospects of war . . . catastrophe . . .*

*A year favouring action and change. Children born in the year of the Tiger will benefit from the light if they are born between sunrise and sunset.*

THE RAT – He won't feel safe this year. Better to stay close to those who like him – and leave the epics to Tigers!

THE BUFFALO – Buffalo will remain anxious, nervy – and dangerous – all the year. Most of the time, they'll stay home, waiting for better days.

THE TIGER – Now Tigers come into their own! They can do whatever they like, for luck is with them. Time to undertake important things, while under this protection . . .

THE CAT – An uneasy year. Those who love tranquillity and calm will hate the changes that threaten their peace.

THE DRAGON – All the brouhaha doesn't worry our carnival beast: it gives him an opportunity to shine . . . and to make himself prettier than ever!

*THE SNAKE* – Goodness, how tiring life is! ... But Snakes are wise and they can draw a lesson from all the fuss.

*THE HORSE* – Will probably take advantage of this year of change to leave home, or split up with a marriage partner. Something is going to change in any case!

*THE GOAT* – What can be done when everyone is spending so much time trying to change the world ... and so little time on the Goat? Poor Goat!

*THE MONKEY* – Time to sit on the sidelines – and laugh. The Monkey watches the events of this year as an amused spectator: he can see the pointlessness of it all.

*THE ROOSTER* – Everything is changing ... how difficult it all is! ... how disagreeable! ... what a hard year this will be!

*THE DOG* – In his element at last, the Dog finds opportunities to display his devotion to Causes. He will be happy for once ...

*THE PIG* – So things are changing ... once again the Pig will adapt. And since Pigs are generous creatures, they won't even find too much to criticize in revolutions.

# THE YEAR OF THE CAT

1951    1963    1975    1987    etc

*This year will seem on the surface to be a calm one. Take the opportunity and rest — for the next may be exhausting! Entertain. Read and gossip in front of the fire . . .*

*A great year for diplomats. Expect changes, especially, in the Law. The aspects are favourable for legal people.*

*Children born in the year of the Cat will be happy and calm if their birthday is in summer.*

*THE RAT* – A time to be careful: the Cat is waiting just round the corner! Better mingle with the crowd and try not to be noticed!

*THE BUFFALO* – Not an ideal year . . . but things are definitely turning for the better. At least one can work in peace!

*THE TIGER* – Take advantage of the prevailing calm and rest a bit. The Cat wishes no harm to Tigers . . .

*THE CAT* – A lovely time to drowse in front of the fire. No problems here for Cats . . . just bring in the friends, have a ball, do good business . . .

*THE DRAGON* – The Cat has no intention of preventing the Dragon from striking his attitudes, from shining in his parade. On the contrary, it will amuse him . . .

*THE SNAKE* – Whew! Time to relax and enjoy a well-earned meal! A successful year for Serpents.

*THE HORSE* – A good year ... romance, work, social life, perhaps even a little politics!

*THE GOAT* – At last, someone is taking notice! Invitations, meetings, parties, people who like the company of Goats! A very good year.

*THE MONKEY* – Excellent for business, the year is favourable for Monkeys from every point of view.

*THE ROOSTER* – Still a bit shattered by the previous year, our Rooster will stay on the defensive and undertake nothing new.

*THE DOG* – Time to take a rest now. But the Dog will be almost happy, just the same, for the Cat brings him peace and quiet. It might be a good idea to profit from this and get married!

*THE PIG* – All will go well – provided there is no hint of anything to do with court cases in the air. These must be avoided at all costs, even if it means a bit of a loss of face.

# THE YEAR OF THE DRAGON

## 1952   1964   1976   1988   etc

*Be ambitious and enterprising this year; push
your way to the front. It's an exhausting year, a
brilliant year, a year of pageants and fêtes; a year
of spectacular victory (or defeat) . . .*

*Be on your guard against fires.*

*The auguries are good for resounding successes,
either militarily or in another field (perhaps
politics). But take care: such victories are in
general illusory!*

*If your child is born in this year, you don't have to
do a thing for him yourself: he's going to be all
right (unless he happened to be born on the day of
a storm — in which case, watch out!).*

THE RAT – This year suits the Rat very well. It's a
year of good business and no anxiety.

THE BUFFALO – Reassured by the pomp and cere-
mony, the Buffalo thinks the good times have come
back. Alas! It's only an illusion – so he'd better get
down to work!

THE TIGER – He, too, can find a lot to like in this
year: it's a year of swagger and panache, and
Tigers adore that!

THE CAT – Watching all the fuss with some

amusement, Cats will stay at home and mind their own business.

*THE DRAGON* – Happy as a fish in the sea! It's the year of his glory!

*THE SNAKE* – Common sense forecasts that there's no need to worry about all this bustle! In reality, everything is calm; all goes well. Life smiles on Snakes!

*THE HORSE* – Not a bad year for the parade-loving Horse. Satisfactions in store.

*THE GOAT* – What with one thing and another, there's a lot of fun to be got from all the fanfares and processions ...

*THE MONKEY* – What fun, what fun! The Monkey's role here is basic, for the Dragon always has need of him.

*THE ROOSTER* – A year made to measure for Roosters. They can preen and strut and flirt to their heart's content. Better still, get married!

*THE DOG* – All the fuss exasperates the Dog. It seems pointless to him. Sullen and a little peevish, he'll keep himself to himself.

*THE PIG* – Convinced that it's possible to live more of a 'real' life than this, the Pig takes refuge among his friends. All the pomp bores him. He eats well and grows fat ...

# THE YEAR OF THE SNAKE

## 1953   1965   1977   1989   etc

*Reflect, flirt, idle away the time . . . this is the
year for lovers and adulterers! If that's your de-
sire, now is the time to act: nobody is taking
notes . . .*

*A year of wisdom on the political and diplomatic
scene. Solutions to all problems.*

*If your child was born under the sign of the Snake,
the hotter it was on the day of his birth, the happier
he will be in life.*

*THE RAT* – A bad year for business. Better to let
it be and use the time to write (all Rats can do this
if they try, and it's a good year for thinkers anyway!).

*THE BUFFALO* – Watch out for trouble in the
home – and with the family! Take care not to let
bad temper get the better of you. Don't be violent.
Buffalo should never marry during the year of the
Snake.

*THE TIGER* – A time for leaving on voyages of
discovery, for finding forgotten tribes and buried
cities . . . Above all, avoid inactivity!

*THE CAT* – A good year. One thinks, one philoso-
phizes, one writes perhaps – and domestic dramas
and traumas stay away from the door . . .

*THE DRAGON* – Everything is for the best. Under the serene eye of the Snake, the Dragon can continue to glitter and shine with all his might.

*THE SNAKE* – It's the Snake's year, of course: anything can be attempted, anything can be done – and without risk, too! Exciting adventures in love.

*THE HORSE* – Once again, everything could be abandoned for the sake of love. It would be a great mistake in this case, however, for the romances of the year of the Snake are short-lived . . .

*THE GOAT* – Fun this year for the Goat, with plenty of interesting and amusing things to do . . . and plenty of scandal to gossip about!

*THE MONKEY* – Such a useful creature will surely find a niche here! In fact, the opportunist Monkey once again makes itself indispensable.

*THE ROOSTER* – A great interest shown in what goes on – but maybe there will be a family problem to solve at home as well.

*THE DOG* – The year of the thinker, the philosopher and the discoverer – and the Dog, naturally, is among those doing the thinking, philosophizing, and discovering. He won't be unhappy!

*THE PIG* – Lucky in business, unlucky in love . . . the year of the Snake, unfortunately, brings with it a stack of romantic problems.

# THE YEAR OF THE HORSE

## 1954  1966*  1978  1990  etc

*Work for everybody . . . think of yourself. Take part in meetings, gatherings, club sessions; interest yourself in politics, sport, the theatre . . .*

*Whatever happens, it's tact and diplomacy that will carry the day. There will be political reverses (not serious ones), resignations, fits of temper, scandals perhaps . . . and of course the backwash from all this. But everything will sort itself out.*

*For horses: a good year on the flat or over the sticks.*

*It is better for the Horse if he is born in winter.*

THE RAT – Catastrophic for the Rat . . . from every point of view. He will fall into debt . . .

THE BUFFALO – Things work out well this year. Business looks up (but the Buffalo must make sure he takes advantage of this).

THE TIGER – It is necessary to start something: idleness must be avoided. There is no danger for the Tiger.

THE CAT – Not a displeasing year, on the whole. Since all seems quiet on all fronts . . . and the Cat knows what he is about . . . well, who knows . . . ?

* 1906, 1966: years of the Fire Horse.

*THE DRAGON* – Once again, an opportunity to walk at the head of the procession . . .

*THE SNAKE* – Watch out for disappointments in love. This year is too emotional by half for the Snake, and he'll need every ounce of his common sense to get himself out of it!

*THE HORSE* – Unlike all the other signs, the Horse's own year is never good for the Horse himself. As for the Fire Horse – well, that year could be tragic.

*THE GOAT* – A good year! All this is so amusing, so convenient, such fun!

*THE MONKEY* – Although competitions and races (on the flat or over the sticks) are not to his taste, the Monkey will nevertheless row himself into a well-paid job . . .

*THE ROOSTER* – All systems go! These incidents, these changes, amuse our feathered friend only to the extent that they do not threaten his security.

*THE DOG* – Irritation . . . The Dog wants to hurl himself into the thick of it – but he's not sufficiently convinced that it'll be a success!

*THE PIG* – Pigs get down to organizing themselves. But the romantic troubles continue just the same! An unfavourable period.

## THE YEAR OF THE GOAT

### 1955 1967 1979 1991 etc —

*Have a few whims of your own! Get out into the country and infest your friends!*

*Politically, financially, this is a year on the brink of catastrophe. But international face will (just) be saved and equilibrium — despite a certain lack of wisdom and competence — will be maintained. We shall muddle through again.*

*A good year for artists in general and actors in particular.*

*Generally speaking, the omens favour Goats born on a day when there is no rain.*

*THE RAT* – A start can be made at last to re-climb the ladder. The Rat could with success devote himself to art this year.

*THE BUFFALO* – A bad year. He will be nervous and sulky.

*THE TIGER* – Better start another round-the-world trip: it's his only chance!

*THE CAT* – The minor disappointments of the year of the Cat cannot threaten the Cat's peace and quiet, and so contentment will reign.

*THE DRAGON* – A year of rest! Dragons would do well to hold themselves aloof from all this incompetence!

*THE SNAKE* – His intelligence finds it impossible to tolerate all this idiocy. He tries to forget it all in a series of amorous adventures.

*THE HORSE* – A bit of rearing between the shafts, here . . . but goodness! how things have improved!

*THE GOAT* – Everything in the garden is lovely! People take notice of the Goat and she sees the promise of a brilliant future. Let's hope she knows how to take advantage of it . . .

*THE MONKEY* – Time to plot, plan, play both ends against the middle . . . and entertain yourself doing so.

*THE ROOSTER* – 'Pinch me in case I'm asleep!' The Rooster never thought this could happen to him. He stirs up a lot of trouble for himself.

*THE DOG* – The mood passes from mere irritation to total exasperation. The Dog risks chucking it all up and (if he is old) finishing his days in splendid solitude.

*THE PIG* – The Pig is full of hope. The scene generally seems to have little importance and little relevance. Finally, all goes well – and romantically, all goes better!

# THE YEAR OF THE MONKEY

## 1956  1968  1980  1992  etc

*Expect anything this year — especially the unexpected! Take risks . . . everything's going to be all right: the Monkey knows when to stop! It's no good trying to be reasonable, to look before you leap. Thinking first is out this year!*

*There are pleasantries for all to enjoy in the year of the Monkey — riots, for instance, or revolutions, or the overthrow of rulers, or even barricades (remember Paris in 1968?). The Monkey will have his little joke! So it's muddle and anarchy all round, with anything liable to happen. But at least nobody will be bored!*

*A good time to launch new ideas, though. Take advantage of it.*

*If you are born this year, try and make it in the summer . . .*

THE RAT – All the jokes amuse the Rat. At last happiness and equilibrium return; the labours of the past bear fruit. A good year to get married.

THE BUFFALO – An extremely bad year. The Buffalo is frightened and feels himself threatened. He can't bear the unexpected.

THE TIGER – He thinks The Time has come . . . and throws all his energy into the furtherance of new and exciting ideas. But the Monkey is laughing behind his hand . . .

*THE CAT* – Cats won't be unduly worried or unduly impressed: they know what the Monkey is and take him as they find him. Quietly, they'll wait until it's all over.

*THE DRAGON* – He puts himself forward again . . . but he's liable to regret it: he can't bear being made fun of!

*THE SNAKE* – Common sense and intelligence tell the Snake that none of this can possibly be taken seriously. But he may join in just the same . . . only to see what it's all about, of course . . . just to satisfy his curiosity.

*THE HORSE* – All great fun, when you come down to it! A time for the Horse to play politics a little . . . carefully, of course. And always leaving his escape route clear . . .

*THE GOAT* – Once again nobody is taking any notice of the Goat! And all this could be amusing – it *would* be amusing, if only it was happening at home. The Goat's home . . . Maybe one should join, just for fun!

*THE MONKEY* – Jubilation, of course! The Monkey himself won't get his feet wet, or not for long: it's so rib-splitting to watch all this chaos from the outside!

*THE ROOSTER* – The Rooster comes over all moralistic and struts about talking pompously and aggressively of 'putting everything in order' again. The world ought to be the way *he* wants it . . . The situation could bring out courage and devotion in him, though.

*THE DOG* – Like the Tiger, the Dog believes that The Day has come. Rushing in at the deep end, he is likely to retire with his tail between his legs – but ready to start again at the drop of a hat!

*THE PIG* – On one side or the other, the Pig does what he thinks is right with all his enthusiasm. Romantically, things take a turn for the better. Suddenly, life is worth living again!

# THE YEAR OF THE ROOSTER

## 1957   1969   1981   1993   etc

*A hard year. It will be necessary to work hard to make a living. Risk of unemployment. Money isn't going to fall into your lap – nor food into the Rooster's beak – without effort.*

*The Rooster isn't going to put up with any nonsense trifling with law and order; there'll be no joking with those who disturb the status quo. A year of reaction, therefore, with an abundance of uniforms in the name of the law – though in fact they are worn for their own sake. Military parades. Reviews. Risks of the abuse of police powers.*

*A good year (as if we didn't know!) for military careers. Now is the time to ask for a medal or buy your way into the Honours List.*

*Young Cocks born in the Spring will be less aggressive.*

THE RAT – Everything goes well for the Rat. The changes in society will not affect him – or very rarely. He thinks only of enjoying life.

THE BUFFALO – At last, one can breathe again! How much better one feels when things are properly under control! The Buffalo turns back to work with renewed vigour.

THE TIGER – Disappointed and unhappy, the

Tiger will be. This will be the year of the true revolt – but the Tiger will plot in secret, though he will voice his opposition openly.

*THE CAT* – An irritating year: the Cat finds the Rooster and his parades ridiculous. Fiercely anti-militarist, the Cat is not at all happy.

*THE DRAGON* – As always, the Dragon improves the shining hour – by finding the opportunity to shine more brightly still! But he's too wise to *act*!

*THE SNAKE* – A hard year. The Snake is by nature idle – and he has to make an effort to survive. There will be many discouragements.

*THE HORSE* – This time, the rear is covered! One can go back to work and put one's back into it! All goes well.

*THE GOAT* – Declining to work (thank you very much!), the Goat lives a 'Bohemian' year, waiting until it's all over.

*THE MONKEY* – It's not so funny now that the year of the Monkey is over – even though the Rooster's efforts are hilarious!

*THE ROOSTER* – The prospect of a splendid year! Hang out the flags at the Rooster's home! ... Unfortunately, though, even the Rooster has to work to live – and it's a hard year. Thank goodness everything is under control, at least, and order reigns once more!

*THE DOG* – Disappointed, like the Tiger, the Dog continues the fight underground. It will be a hard year, nevertheless.

*THE PIG* – The Pig finds that his work really pays off this year. Everything goes well for him. Life is good ...

# THE YEAR OF THE DOG

1958   1970   1982   1994   etc

*You'll be pessimistic, anxious, and worrying about your future. You'll be on the defensive all the time – but full of generosity and good-will too.*

*A year with plenty of political action. Things veer suddenly towards a more liberal approach. Idealism. Possibility of revolution.*

*A year, in fact, favourable to the Left, to grandiose schemes and to disinterested, generous acts.*

*For children born this year, it is better not to be born at night. Those who are, ceaselessly on the alert, will stay that way for the rest of their lives . . .*

*THE RAT* – If he can bear to pay attention to his business affairs rather than to his love affairs, this should be a good year for the Rat . . .

*THE BUFFALO* – Not a good year for the Buffalo. In every way, he sees everything going to the Dogs! The future seems gloomy . . . and as for the young people today . . . !

*THE TIGER* – A little anxious still, but ready for anything and full of enterprise. The great Causes can count on the Tiger!

*THE CAT* – Cats are a little uneasy, too. Take the necessary precautions and play at politics a bit . . .

*THE DRAGON* – The Dragon can do anything! He will always be ready to act; generous, skilful, perfect – but . . .

*THE SNAKE* – Once again a year of uncertainties and unease. The Snake is sure of nothing . . . not even his own feelings! He'd like very much to have some changes made . . . but he's too lazy to act.

*THE HORSE* – Too selfish and self-centred to worry on behalf of others, the Horse will work on doggedly for his own well-being.

*THE GOAT* – A bad year again . . . everyone is far too preoccupied with their own affairs to spare a thought for the Goats of this world. The Goats therefore feel neglected . . .

*THE MONKEY* – Too intelligent to feel really worried, the Monkey waits patiently for the end . . . of certain financial difficulties!

*THE ROOSTER* – The parade is over! The Rooster is flaked out! And unfortunately for him the year brings severe financial difficulties . . .

*THE DOG* – The Dog triumphs . . . but modestly. He doesn't believe in Father Christmas – but he knows that every effort is worth the trouble of taking.

*THE PIG* – Financially, things continue well. The Pig is not unhappy. A period, in fact, of peace and quiet. The Pig approves in general of the Dog's actions – though he doesn't take part in any himself.

# THE YEAR OF THE PIG

## 1959   1971   1983   1995   etc

*All's for the best in the best of all possible worlds!
Business is good. Money circulates again. One
savours the joy of living.*

*A time of surplus. Certain minor administrative
difficulties.*

*A good year for intellectuals as well as for
financiers.*

*If you could arrange the birthdate of your child,
the time to avoid would be just before the* Four de
Têt (*New Year*) *– for Piglets born then, nicely
fattened, may well be consumed as part of the
festivities!*

THE RAT – All goes well, very well . . . The Rat is
   happy to be alive. He makes plans for the future.
THE BUFFALO – This should be a better year.
   There's plenty of work about – but there is
   trouble to overcome.
THE TIGER – Good business! Risking everything
   on a single throw will pay dividends . . . provided
   the luck lasts!
THE CAT – Calmed, the Cat purrs and looks up his
   friends again. Business is good. He feels secure and
   contented.

*THE DRAGON* – He glitters! Certainly, *he* has never been short of a penny, but this year – thanks to his shrewdness – things are particularly good!

*THE SNAKE* – Nothing is perfect . . . but the Snake will accept what's coming to him. After all, he's wise – and he can wait for a year of a better vintage!

*THE HORSE* – The Horse will have money wherever he goes! . . . and perhaps at last he will be able to realize a dream he has had secretly for ages – a new car, perhaps, or an apartment . . .

*THE GOAT* – The prosperity of others will bring happiness to Goats in so far as they can see a way to profit by it themselves. Useless to recommend prudence: Goats don't know the meaning of the word!

*THE MONKEY* – End of the change in fortune brought by the previous year. Business looks up. The Monkey is let loose again . . .

*THE ROOSTER* – Lots of work to do! The Rooster begins the laborious re-ascent of the financial slope. He's had enough of working his fingers to the bone for damn-all! Yet, against his own interest, he remains staunchly conservative . . .

*THE DOG* – The Dog ponders a little, this year, about his well-being – and about his family. They'd better make hay while the sun shines, because it won't last!

*THE PIG* – The year belongs to him! Everything he touches turns to gold! He will be happy in love and fortunate in business. He could find that he'd unexpectedly been left money, or come in for a large sum in some other way . . .

# What They Should Be

## THE RAT

Shopkeeper, second-hand dealer, commercial traveller, official (important or minor).

Accountant, publicist, businessman.

Or perhaps: musician, painter, writer.

Or even: pawnbroker, prostitute, moneylender, crook, and . . . critic!


## THE BUFFALO

Farm labourer, farmer, mechanic, garage hand.

Skilled workman, technician, craftsman.

Draughtsman or architect, photographer.

Receptionist, nurse, cook, hairdresser.

Dental mechanic. Surgeon.

And also: sergeant-major, dictator, and . . . cop!


## THE TIGER

Foreman, head parachutist, gang boss, head of department, Head of State, matador, chief driver in racing team, chief stunt-man, chief explorer, military chief, revolutionary chief, mercenaries' chief . . . and anything else that begins with 'chief' – not excluding Indian Chief.

## THE CAT

Model girl, dressmaker, couturier, decorator (interior), antiquary, receptionist, shopkeeper (pharmacist or beautician).

Publicist, press relations officer, actor.

Solicitor, barrister, notary public, magistrate, judge.

Stockbroker, speculator, diplomat, ambassador . . . and landlord.

## THE DRAGON

Actor, artist.

Industrialist, shopkeeper, architect, doctor, barrister.

Gangster, priest, prophet.

Ambassador, politician, director-general, managing director, President . . . and national hero!

## THE SNAKE

Headmaster, university professor.

Writer, philosopher, jurist, psychiatrist, alienist.

Politician, diplomat, stockbroker.

But also: soothsayer, clairvoyant, seer, fortune-teller, necromancer, medium, crystal ball-gazer, astrologer, palmist, calligraphist, etc.

## THE HORSE

Skilled craftsman, technician, long-distance lorry-driver, foreman.

Chemist, geologist, physicist, biologist, etc. Dentist,

doctor. Architect. Financier, diplomat, politician, painter, or poet.

Adventurer, explorer, cosmonaut.

But also: barman or hairdresser.

## THE GOAT

Artisan, technician, gardener.

Actor, artist (theatre, cinema, photography, literature, poetry, painting, music, vaudeville, etc).

But also: gigolo, courtesan, parasite, pimp, ponce, callgirl, man of straw, beachcomber, tramp.

Or: person retired to the country (at the house of friends).

## THE MONKEY

It doesn't matter what (so long as the Monkey thinks it worth while taking the trouble).

Genial speculator or stockbroker, redoubtable businessman, famous writer, film-maker in fashion, with-it shopkeeper, subtle diplomat, shrewd politician.

And also: irresistible crook and con-man.

## THE ROOSTER

Café waiter, cook, bar owner.

Traveller, public relations man.

Beautician, woman's hairdresser, dentist, surgeon.

And also: white-collar worker, soldier, fireman, night-watchman, policeman.

But in addition: bodyguard, torpedo, strong-arm man . . . and dancing partner.

## THE DOG

Union activist, industrialist, foreman.

Critic, educator, priest.

Writer, philosopher, thinker, moralist, judge, magistrate with integrity, doctor, scientist, scholar.

Objective politician, secret agent, power behind throne.

But above all: right-hand man for left-wing politician.

## THE PIG

Manufacturer, doctor, scientist, architect, filmmaker, writer, poet, painter, businessman.

But also: public entertainer (variety artist, clown, comedian, pop star).

# Compatibility Tables

*What kind of friendship will there be between . . .*

. . . Rat and Rat:
> All right – but neither will be able to resist the temptation to play dirty tricks on the other.

. . . Buffalo and Rat:
> Pooh! *They* don't have many things to talk about!

. . . Buffalo and Buffalo:
> None. There is a conflict of authority here.

. . . Tiger and Rat:
> None. The Tiger is an idealist and the Rat is a materialist.

. . . Tiger and Buffalo:
> None. The Buffalo breed is not recommended for Tigers. They give them indigestion!

. . . Tiger and Tiger:
> Let them take each other on motor racing, tour the world together, start a revolution – anything *but* live together under the same roof!

. . . Cat and Rat:
> None. The Cat always holds a definite opinion about the Rat . . . and it's not exactly friendly!

. . . Cat and Buffalo:

Good relations socially.

. . . Cat and Tiger:

They understand each other very well. But the Cat won't take the Tiger seriously, and the Tiger resents it.

. . . Cat and Cat:

Yes, yes, yes! Just think of all those days spent gossiping by the fire!

. . . Dragon and Rat:

This could be . . . because they appreciate each other. And it's not the Rat who tries to shine at the expense of the Dragon!

. . . Dragon and Buffalo:

No. The Buffalo doesn't think much of Dragons.

. . . Dragon and Tiger:

Yes. They complement one another and are, in general, very useful to each other.

. . . Dragon and Cat:

Hah! Yes, yes . . . No more to be said!

. . . Dragon and Dragon:

When two fireworks go off together, neither can dazzle the audience!

. . . Snake and Rat:

Okay, for they have much to tell each other. A gossipy friendship!

... Snake and Buffalo:
> There's a lot of difference between them, but they get on well enough.

... Snake and Tiger:
> No: it would be like a conversation of deaf mutes.

... Snake and Cat:
> Yes. They will have long, stimulating conversations together.

... Snake and Dragon:
> Yes. They will get on well together, each setting the other off.

... Snake and Snake:
> Another happy relationship ... two philosophers putting the world right!

... Horse and Rat:
> The question simply doesn't arise. They don't get on.

... Horse and Buffalo:
> Neither their tastes nor their attitudes to life coincide.

... Horse and Tiger:
> They will argue all night – but they're fond of one another for all that!

... Horse and Cat:
> Excellent relations socially ... and maybe real friendship too.

... Horse and Dragon:
> No. The Horse, too self-centred, expects a lot but gives little. The Dragon gives a lot and expects a lot in return.

... Horse and Snake:
> Yes. The Horse's raging will slide off the Snake's back!

... Horse and Horse:
> Fine. Each will respect the independence of the other.

... Goat and Rat:
> It wouldn't last long! A flash in the pan!

... Goat and Buffalo:
> They won't put up with each other – or not for long.

... Goat and Tiger:
> Difficult to see what they could achieve together. The Goat thinks ideas up; the Tiger puts them into action.

... Goat and Cat:
> Yes. The Cat admires the Goat's artistic sense – and those whims just amuse him!

... Goat and Dragon:
> Oh yes! The Goat will be so flattered that she will turn on the charm! And when the Goat does turn on the charm ...

... Goat and Snake:
> Possible ... as long as the Snake will lend the
> Goat a helping hand.

... Goat and Horse:
> Yes. It's such fun gambolling on the edge of a
> precipice!

... Goat and Goat:
> Goats get on well together – though they don't
> *rely* on each other too much!

... Monkey and Rat:
> Yes – but always at the expense of the Rat.

... Monkey and Buffalo:
> The Buffalo likes the Monkey ... if only he
> wouldn't tease so!

... Monkey and Tiger:
> The charm of the Monkey makes the relation-
> ship an interesting one – though it is to the
> advantage of neither to deepen it.

... Monkey and Cat:
> Two good friends, two accomplices ... better
> to leave well enough alone!

... Monkey and Dragon:
> The Monkey does what he likes with the
> Dragon. But the Dragon can make use of the
> Monkey!

... Monkey and Snake:
Social relations without warmth.

... Monkey and Horse:
No. The Horse distrusts the Monkey ...
rightly!

... Monkey and Goat:
Yes. The Monkey will like the Goat because
they will never be bored together.

... Monkey and Monkey:
They'll have a marvellous time together – always at the expense of others. Remarkable!

... Rooster and Rat:
An acquaintance only, perhaps. They're only
superficially on each other's wavelength.

... Rooster and Buffalo:
They can form a lifelong friendship together.

... Rooster and Tiger:
They probably haven't tried; the idea doesn't
appeal.

... Rooster and Cat:
No. The Rooster is too brash. The Cat would
be tired out.

... Rooster and Dragon:
They are in harmony – and that's it!

. . . Rooster and Snake:
     Yes! They have a lot to say to each other!

. . . Rooster and Horse:
     Good social relations. Parties, dances, teas.

. . . Rooster and Goat:
     Impossible! The Rooster is too much of
     a stick-in-the-mud, despite his strutting.
     There's something about the Goat that he
     can't make out.

. . . Rooster and Monkey:
     They have nothing in common. The Rooster
     would end up by exploding!

. . . Rooster and Rooster:
     Battles assured! Friendship out of the question!

. . . Dog and Rat:
     No. The Rat doesn't aim high enough for the
     Dog.

. . . Dog and Buffalo:
     Difficult to conceive of a friendship here.

. . . Dog and Tiger:
     There couldn't be a more solid friendship.

. . . Dog and Cat:
     Yes. The Cat will at least lend a sympathetic
     ear to the Dog – even if she doesn't actually
     offer any real help.

... Dog and Dragon:
> No. The Dog is too much of a realist and the Dragon is discouraged.

... Dog and Snake:
> Difficult. Best to leave it at a strictly social level.

... Dog and Horse:
> They'll talk politics, of course. And if they agree ... why not?

... Dog and Goat:
> Not really. They can only put up with each other with difficulty.

... Dog and Monkey:
> Perhaps ... who knows? But the Monkey isn't one to give praise lightly.

... Dog and Rooster:
> There's a barrier between them ... a fence, a wall, a ditch ... a world!

... Dog and Dog:
> Two good friends – but it will hardly be the gayest of relationships!

... Pig and Rat:
> Two good mates who enjoy going out together and having a bit of a joke. But the aggressiveness of the Rat finds no echo in the Pig.

... Pig and Buffalo:
> Yes – as long as they don't see each other too often!

... Pig and Tiger:
> Yes – they get on well together. But the Pig will have to be careful.

... Pig and Cat:
> Yes ... as long as they never go out together: the Pig's truculence might shock the Cat.

... Pig and Dragon:
> Plain sailing. No problems, certainly – but no fun either!

... Pig and Snake:
> Maybe yes, maybe no: only time will tell.

... Pig and Horse:
> The Pig will be reticent. And he will be right.

... Pig and Goat:
> Yes. The Pig knows how to deal with Goats, and he's fond of them, too!

... Pig and Monkey:
> Two good friends here, for the Monkey respects the Pig!

... Pig and Rooster:
> The Pig would do better to make the Rooster keep his distance.

... Pig and Dog:
> These two are absolutely devoted. The Pig helps the Dog take his mind off his anxieties.

... Pig and Pig:
> The same tastes, of course. Two inseparable companions, soldiers from the same regiment who go out drinking and carousing together.

*What kind of love will there be ...*

*If she's a Rat ...*

... and he's a Rat:
> Two Rats love one another with an especially tender affection. What a love affair! Like this, the rest of the world can go hang!

... and he's a Buffalo:
> A hundred times yes! Undisturbed bliss! The Rat can love in peace and quiet.

... and he's a Tiger:
> Hmn ... But as long as the Rat allows the Tiger to have his little adventures, nothing stands in the way of their Diamond Wedding.

... and he's a Cat:
> The Rat will be permanently in danger ... because the Cat likes to stay at his place – and finds it difficult to resist the temptation to destroy her host!

... and he's a Dragon:
> Good. The Rat can be useful to the Dragon – and the Dragon admits it.

... and he's a Snake:
> In the final analysis, this is a risk that could be taken ... but the Rat falls in love so blindly!

... and he's a Horse:
> No! Too many emotional problems. No good could come of it.

... and he's a Goat:
> B'rrrr! Don't try it! Your curiosity will be punished!

... and he's a Monkey:
> One of the best combinations. Lady Rat adores Lord Monkey. They'll be happy.

... and he's a Rooster:
> They'll end up on the floor!

... and he's a Dog:
> Why not? The Rat can bring a breath of sentimentality and realism to the idealistic world of the Dog.

... and he's a Pig:
> Good. They'll make it if the Rat controls his aggression. The Pig's not a fan of that kind of force.

*If she's a Buffalo . . .*

... and he's a Rat:
> A couple of good ones. The woman wears the
> trousers – but she is faithful and realistic and
> she'll make the Rat happy.

... and he's a Buffalo:
> Materialistic and conservative, they'll end up
> calling each other Mum and Dad!

... and he's a Tiger:
> Not at any price. The Tiger would be finished –
> he'd better watch out!

... and he's a Cat:
> Yes ... Perhaps. Why not? The Cat man can
> laugh at himself being ordered about.

... and he's a Dragon:
> No. There'd be a continuous fight over who
> was boss. And the Dragon would get bored.

... and he's a Snake:
> Yes. The Snake leaves the decisions to the
> Buffalo, and he'll always be discreet – and
> always there!

... and he's a Horse:
> The lady Buffalo is dominating ... the selfish
> Horse is independent. They will part.

. . . and he's a Goat:
> Bad! The Buffalo lady will end up by showing master Goat to the door – with no regrets!

. . . and he's a Monkey:
> The Buffalo loves the Monkey – and the Monkey is clever enough to ease himself out of this family complex.

. . . and he's a Rooster:
> This would be perfect as long as the vain Rooster didn't attempt to be boss – or make it look that way! Self control, please!

. . . and he's a Dog:
> Difficult . . . but possible. As long as the Buffalo lady contents herself with running a home.

. . . and he's a Pig:
> H'mn . . . The Pig will look elsewhere for the satisfactions he cannot find at home. There'll be trouble for him . . .

*If she's a Tiger . . .*

. . . and he's a Rat:
> No future in this. The Tiger lady dreams of *la Dolce Vita* and the poor Rat knocks himself out trying to please her.

. . . and he's a Buffalo:

> Impossible. They couldn't live together be-
> cause the Buffalo would finish the Tiger. She'd
> have no life at all.

. . . and he's a Tiger:

> Even if they get on well together – and it's
> likely they would – living under the same roof
> is definitely not advised.

. . . and he's a Cat:

> Difficult. The female Tiger is a complex crea-
> ture – but the Cat man is flexible . . . and a
> scoffer!

. . . and he's a Dragon:

> Yes – and never mind the difficulties. The
> Dragon knows how to reason with the Tiger,
> who will listen to his advice . . . even when it's
> bad!

. . . and he's a Snake:

> They don't look at anything with the same
> eye. Difficult to see what they could see in
> each other.

. . . and he's a Horse:

> Why not? If the Tiger lady can find a 'cause'
> to advance, the Horse can enjoy an agreeable
> and peaceful life!

. . . and he's a Goat:

> Ai-ai-ai . . . Ninety per cent sure that the Tiger
> will end up by devouring the Goat!

... and he's a Monkey:

> Not too easy! The Monkey man risks turning the female Tiger into a bitch!

... and he's a Rooster:

> No. The Tiger lady cannot put up with the fatuity of the Rooster, and so she'll be unfair to him.

... and he's a Dog:

> Yes ... if a little crazy! They are both out of this world a bit!

... and he's a Pig:

> Why not? Just as long as the Tiger, without knowing it, doesn't take advantage of the Pig's good nature.

*If she's a Cat ...*

... and he's a Rat:

> Though she's a quiet one, the female Cat always runs the risk of devouring the Rat. Rats who are not masochists abstain, therefore!

... and he's a Buffalo:

> This could work. They're not tailored for each other, but the female Cat is patient, tactful – and a bit of a tartar!

... and he's a Tiger:

It would be stretching it a bit, but they understand one another. And the female Cat knows how to hold her own with the Tiger.

... and he's a Cat:

Why not, as long as they are both grown up! (This would be an ideal union for homosexuals – perhaps in an antique shop!)

... and he's a Dragon:

A very good team. The social assets of the Cat, and her tact, will further the Dragon's ambitions.

... and he's a Snake:

Uh uh ... perhaps yes ... as long as it's in slippers (the bitter end for a Snake!) and by the fireside!

... and he's a Horse:

Fine, fine. The Cat will stay at home in the warm, surrounded by friends. As far as she's concerned, that's enough!

... and he's a Goat:

Why not? If the Cat has a little money, they can at least stay friends – even if there's no love there.

... and he's a Monkey:

A nice little suburban home – provided the Monkey keeps himself under control.

... and he's a Rooster:

>Not at any price. Even if they are not important, the Cat will be exasperated by the Rooster's excesses.

... and he's a Dog:

>Yes – if a little mad. The female Cat will bring the Dog peace and quiet, a little serenity, some good advice, a home.

... and he's a Pig:

>All will go well – as long as the Cat can put up with a bit of smut! But the Pig must be able to find consolations elsewhere without the Cat finding fault.

## If she's a Dragon ...

... and he's a Rat:

>Why not? Lady Dragons adore to be adored, and who knows how to adore better than an adoring Rat!

... and he's a Buffalo:

>Conflict! The Dragon likes to shine – and the Buffalo mistrusts anything bright.

... and he's a Tiger:

>Two strong characters face to face. The female

Dragon will be useful to the Tiger, bringing him both prudence and the quality of looking before he leaps.

. . . and he's a Cat:

If they must . . . as long as the female Dragon doesn't get too bored staying in by the fire all the time.

. . . and he's a Dragon:

A real firework display! They'll be perpetually in competition.

. . . and he's a Snake:

Difficult! The Dragon likes to be courted, complimented, adored – not ensnared!

. . . and he's a Horse:

No. The Horse is too much of an egoist. And since the lady Dragon needs somebody's full attention before she blossoms . . .

. . . and he's a Goat:

Absolutely not! Dragon ladies need to admire and be admired. The Goat man admires nothing.

. . . and he's a Monkey:

Possible. The male Monkey is such a good actor! He has so much charm! As usual, he'll be disappointed, but he won't show it.

. . . and he's a Rooster:

Yes – if the Dragon has a glamorous job and

the Rooster can take advantage of it to cut a fine caper.

**... and he's a Dog:**

No – the Dog's not a man to admire things blindly: he has better things to do.

**... and he's a Pig:**

Yes. The Pig will fawn upon the Dragon. So much the worse for him!

*If she's a Snake ...*

**... and he's a Rat:**

She'll be happy, though frequently unfaithful. So he'll be unhappy.

**... and he's a Buffalo:**

If the Snake lady can manage to conceal her extra-marital adventures, all will go well. She'll do her best. But if by chance she is found out ...

**... and he's a Tiger:**

Not advised at all. Complete misunderstanding without hope of redemption. Wisdom and enthusiasm make bad bedfellows.

**... and he's a Cat:**

Why not? They can ponder together! And

these two thinking beings will have the leisure
to think of each other.

... and he's a Dragon:
> A good match. The Dragon will be proud of
> the charm of his lady – even if it's not always
> directed at him.

... and he's a Snake:
> Complicated! Adventures, flirtations, affairs
> of the heart ... and continuous attempts to
> put something over on the other!

... and he's a Horse:
> If it makes the Snake lady happy, and if she
> has enough wisdom to allow her to put up with
> such an existence.

... and he's a Goat:
> Wisdom won't help here. There's a risk of the
> whole thing falling by the wayside.

... and he's a Monkey:
> Perhaps. If God (and the Monkey) wills. It all
> depends on the Monkey (and on God!).

... and he's a Rooster:
> Why not? They complement each other well
> enough, and the Snake always has enough
> wisdom not to lose face in front of others.

... and he's a Dog:
> Could be ... provided the Snake lady doesn't
> ask too much.

... and he's a Pig:
> Poor Porker! He'll be inhibited ... and even his taste for dirty jokes will be squashed!

## If she's a Horse ...

... and he's a Rat:
> Sparks will fly! Emotionalism, passion, divorce! This way for the classic *crime passionel*! To be avoided, in fact.

... and he's a Buffalo:
> Difficult. They don't really understand each other. The female Horse, independent and emotional, fears the Buffalo. She'll suffer.

... and he's a Tiger:
> Good. The female Horse can slake her thirst for passion and still remain independent: the Tiger has so many other things to do!

... and he's a Cat:
> Perhaps ... if the Horse doesn't weary of the affair. But the Cat could remain a firm friend, even if she did.

... and he's a Dragon:
> All systems go! Provided it lasts, of course.

... and he's a Snake:

> The Horse is amorous – but faithful. When love has gone, the Horse goes too. The unfaithful Snake will stay at home. They will not be happy.

... and he's a Horse:

> These two tempestuous lovers will be saved by their egoism.

... and he's a Goat:

> To be avoided if the female Horse has no money. If she's well heeled, they could be happy.

... and he's a Monkey:

> No. The Horse needs a healthy emotional life and mistrusts cunning and guile in his love affairs.

... and he's a Rooster:

> No. She'd lose the man among the fine feathers! For her, love is a serious thing.

... and he's a Dog:

> Yes. While the Dog devotes his life to a great Cause, the Horse devotes hers to him ... so everybody is happy!

... and he's a Pig:

> The Pig will suffer from the selfishness of the Horse – whose passion he will never be able to satisfy.

*If she's a Goat . . .*

. . . and he's a Rat:
> If the Rat has a well-stuffed wallet, the Goat will be satisfied – but not the Rat, whose liberty she takes along with that wallet!

. . . and he's a Buffalo:
> The Buffalo cannot stand imagination and will not tolerate at any price the wearing of horns! They'd be unhappy.

. . . and he's a Tiger:
> Bad. In a moment of anger, the Tiger could finish the Goat.

. . . and he's a Cat:
> Good. The Cat likes the Goat's flights of fancy. They share an artistic approach that brings them together.

. . . and he's a Dragon:
> The Goat will be all right. As for the Dragon, not only will she fail to help his career: she'll actually be harmful to him. She couldn't care less.

. . . and he's a Snake:
> The Goat will mend her ways – if the Snake is rich enough. But what a performance!

. . . and he's a Horse:
> Good. They won't bore each other: there'll be

· problems enough to keep the Horse in love, and the Goat will enjoy the security.

... and he's a Goat:

A beatnik's life! What will they live on while they wait for a rich patron or the bailiffs? Lassitude, luckily!

... and he's a Monkey:

If the Monkey is loaded, why not? She'll keep him amused, after all!

... and he's a Rooster:

No. The Goat isn't used to living off love and water. Working's not her business – and watching *him* work just bores her.

... and he's a Dog:

No! Which of them would have the first nervous breakdown?

... and he's a Pig:

As the Pig often enough has plenty of money, the Goat's happy. But how long will it be before he can get her under control?

*If she's a Monkey* ...

... and he's a Rat:

The Monkey will be happy with the Rat. The

Rat is fascinated by the Monkey and will forgive her anything.

... and he's a Buffalo:

The Buffalo loves the Monkey. He, too, will make plenty of concessions – but although he forgives, he will suffer.

... and he's a Tiger:

Difficult ... but it might work if the Tiger goes off on his adventures. She will always know how to charm him back.

... and he's a Cat:

Amusing – though often at other people's expense. They find great pleasure in each other.

... and he's a Dragon:

Good. The Monkey will always have good advice for the over-confident Dragon – and in exchange, the Dragon will protect her.

... and he's a Snake:

Only intelligence and cleverness could save such a union. And even then ...

... and he's a Horse:

Not advised. They'll never understand each other.

... and he's a Goat:

The Monkey could probably get away with

it. But would she ever have the idiocy to contemplate teaming up with a Goat?

... and he's a Monkey:
> Total complicity here. They could go far.

... and he's a Rooster:
> The Monkey can get a lot from the Rooster, but the bird will be unhappy – and the Monkey will remain unsatisfied.

... and he's a Dog:
> Maybe ... with reservations. They are both cynical and without illusion.

... and he's a Pig:
> Why ever not? The Monkey admires the Pig.

*If she's a Rooster ...*

... and he's a Rat:
> M'hm'n ... But the amorous Rat is patient, and though she's a spendthrift Madam Rooster has some good qualities.

... and he's a Buffalo:
> Perfect accord. The Rooster scintillates in peace – at the heart of her family!

. . . and he's a Tiger:

>Lady bird will be outshone by her Tiger. She'll not know what to do.

. . . and he's a Cat:

>The Cat won't want to put up with the Rooster's air in 'his' house. And the lady will make scenes because she likes to go out.

. . . and he's a Dragon:

>Good. The Rooster profits from the Dragon's success – which becomes hers!

. . . and he's a Snake:

>Omens favourable. They'll play philosophers together. And one complements the other.

. . . and he's a Horse:

>If they must . . . but not for always. The Rooster will get hurt.

. . . and he's a Goat:

>Not advised. They'll both be unhappy. . . even if they pretend.

. . . and he's a Monkey:

>The Monkey can make fun of the Rooster all the time – and the Rooster will never catch on. That's what's important!

. . . and he's a Rooster:

>Life would be impossible! Scenes and tantrums guaranteed all the time.

... and he's a Dog:
> Only if it's absolutely necessary. Let the lady organize tea parties and bridge games, and all may be well!

... and he's a Pig:
> The Pig is patient, tolerant, even indulgent. It could work.

## *If she's a Dog . . .*

... and he's a Rat:
> Interesting. It could work if the Rat is not too often at home. The female Dog will hover if he is.

... and he's a Buffalo:
> Some difficulty here. The Dog is a rebel and the Buffalo a reactionary. They don't think the same way about things.

... and he's a Tiger:
> This could be good. They would share the same ideals, fight the same battles. But they might forget to love each other.

... and he's a Cat:
> Fine, as long as they keep it cool. But every time the Dog devotes herself to a Cause, life will become impossible for the Cat.

... and he's a Dragon:

> The Dog, too much of a realist, will see the
> proud Dragon as he really is. And will dis-
> courage him. So they'll both be unhappy.

... and he's a Snake:

> The Snake can do his own thing. And if the
> Dog is enslaved by him, she won't care any-
> way.

... and he's a Horse:

> Yes, why not? Preoccupied with her ideals, the
> Dog will gladly give her independence to the
> Horse ... and she's not jealous.

... and he's a Goat:

> No! This would be too much! They're both
> too pessimistic. It would be sad.

... and he's a Monkey:

> Not advised. The Dog would suffer. She's too
> much of an idealist.

... and he's a Rooster:

> No. The Dog's not very good at suffering fools.
> Her cynicism would out.

... and he's a Dog:

> Yes ... but they're too cool altogether, and
> they'd have money troubles.

... and he's a Pig:

> Great. Love based on mutual understanding
> and esteem.

*If she's a Pig . . .*

. . . and he's a Rat:
> Good. Gamblers and intellectuals at the same time, the Rat and the Pig could be happy together.

. . . and he's a Buffalo:
> The Pig will put up with anything . . . except austerity. And, in the long run, she's always the courage to start again.

. . . and he's a Tiger:
> The Pig understands and esteems the Tiger. The Tiger risks exhausting her, but she's big enough to look after herself.

. . . and he's a Cat:
> Good, very good – as long as the Pig controls that love of low life!

. . . and he's a Dragon:
> Yes. The Pig knows how to flatter and charm. She's so nice, and she wants so much to please!

. . . and he's a Snake:
> Good old Pig! Poor old Pig! She'll end up by being suffocated.

. . . and he's a Horse:
> The Horse, egoist that he is, takes advantage of the Pig. She'll be unhappy.

... and he's a Goat:

As long as he doesn't go beyond all bounds, the Pig will put up with the Goat. The Goat, thus, will become impossible.

... and he's a Monkey:

This could work. It's so easy to put one over on a Pig that the Monkey can't be bothered: it would give him no pleasure. Besides, he thinks a lot of the Pig.

... and he's a Rooster:

Too forceful, the Rooster tires the Pig out. They're not well matched.

... and he's a Dog:

Good. The Pig's love of living balances the Dog's asceticism. Both of them are generous – and, as we know, the Pig is often rich.

... and he's a Pig:

A good match. They'll both make concessions – and they'll get on famously.

*How they get on if the parent is a Rat . . .*

... and the child's a Rat:

A few disputes of little account – but all's well that ends well!

. . . and the child's a Buffalo:

Okay. Whatever the Rat says, the Buffalo will lend an ear.

. . . and the child's a Tiger:

Father Rat can contribute nothing at all for Baby Tiger.

. . . and the child's a Cat:

The Rat parents are frightened of their Cat child – with reason!

. . . and the child's a Dragon:

The Rats will be outshone; the Dragon will be condescending.

. . . and the child's a Snake:

The Snake will have it all his own way – but so nicely and with such charm.

. . . and the child's a Horse:

The Horse will rear up in the shafts. He'll leave home very young because Father (or Mother) Rat gets on his nerves so much.

. . . and the child's a Goat:

Oh-oh! . . . But Father Rat can always see the point of view of a Goat daughter.

. . . and the child's a Monkey:

Baby Monkey will be adored and spoiled, especially if the child is a boy and it's the Mother who is a Rat. But is this a good thing?

... and the child's a Rooster:
> H'mn ... Lots of arguments here. But they'll get there in the end. That Rooster's *such* a nice boy.

... and the child's a Dog:
> Incomprehension! There's not a single idea in common. The Dog will do his duty, nevertheless, as always.

... and the child's a Pig:
> They could be accomplices – especially Father and Daughter. And the Rat's aggression falls a bit flat!

*If the parent is a Buffalo ...*

... and the child's a Rat:
> The Buffalo is bossy and the Rat's aggressive – but they get on famously.

... and the child's a Buffalo:
> Problems of authority here! The child revolts, but ends by obeying!

... and the child's a Tiger:
> Impossible! The Tiger must get out as soon as possible, or the Buffalo – Mother or Father – will destroy him.

. . . and the child's a Cat:

>The Cat's a diplomat. It laughs at authority
>but pretends to obey!

. . . and the child's a Dragon:

>No – the Dragon tends to regard those re-
>sponsible for his existence as idiots (especially
>if it's the Father who is a Buffalo).

. . . and the child's a Snake:

>The Snake is smart enough to do what he's
>told – or seem to.

. . . and the child's a Horse:

>No! The Horse can't stand being told what to
>do. He'll be off – for ever!

. . . and the child's a Goat:

>A hundred times no! Discontented Buffalo plus
>unhappy Goat equals a mess!

. . . and the child's a Monkey:

>Yes – the Buffalo allows himself to be twisted
>around the Monkey's finger.

. . . and the child's a Rooster:

>Yes – the Rooster will put up with authority if
>he's allowed to strut.

. . . and the child's a Dog:

>No. They will get on each other's nerves. The
>Buffalo cannot tolerate people who stand up to
>him and argue.

... and the child's a Pig:
> The Pig likes to help – but he's not very good
> at putting up with a higher authority that must
> be blindly obeyed. He'll rebel.

## If the parent is a Tiger ...

... and the child's a Rat:
> The Tiger couldn't care less what the Rat does.

... and the child's a Buffalo:
> Better for the Tiger to arrange to get rid of the
> Buffalo who will destroy him (boarding
> school? relatives?). The Tiger will suffer.

... and the child's a Tiger:
> Two Tigers cannot live under the same roof!
> (Tiger parents are advised to think seriously
> about The Pill in the Year of the Tiger).

... and the child's a Cat:
> The obedient-seeming Cat will in reality be
> sticking up two fingers!

... and the child's a Dragon:
> Everything in favour of this combination for
> bringing out the best in the child!

... and the child's a Snake:

>Total misunderstanding, though the Snake makes praiseworthy efforts.

... and the child's a Horse:

>Sparks fly between these two headstrong types – but there's plenty of love and respect as well.

... and the child's a Goat:

>The Goat, too often punished, will be unable to flourish in such a strict atmosphere.

... and the child's a Monkey:

>The Tiger will often be made fun of – but the Monkey had better watch out that it doesn't go too far!

... and the child's a Rooster:

>This baby chick doesn't make too much impression on the Tiger – but the Tiger makes plenty on the young Rooster!

... and the child's a Dog:

>Ideal! Idyllic! A perfect accord that will last through ruin, disaster, and even until death if necessary.

... and the child's a Pig:

>Even if the Tiger *is* pig-headed, the Pig will forgive a lot because he is so generous.

*If the parent is a Cat . . .*

. . . and the child's a Rat:
> The Cat plays with the mouse. And while the Cat's away . . .! So the chances of success are (shall we say?) slim.

. . . and the child's a Buffalo:
> The Cat regards this strange child with astonishment – and anxiety. In fact the Cat can't stop teasing the child.

. . . and the child's a Tiger:
> Not too bad. A sense of humour – even if it does mean wounding the Tiger in his self-respect – will go a long way!

. . . and the Child's a Cat:
> How well they'll get on together! No problems here!

. . . and the child's a Dragon:
> On one condition (that the Dragon leaves well enough alone at home and doesn't fuss), the Cat is prepared to tolerate the brilliance of its child.

. . . and the child's a Snake:
> It'll do. There'll be a lot of talk and they'll end up friends. These fraternal relations will please the Cat.

... and the child's a Horse:
> The Cat is known for his peaceful nature. Why can't he let the Horse have his own way?

... and the child's a Goat:
> Good for the Goat! The Cat helps, understands – and admires!

... and the child's a Monkey:
> Baby Monkey knows who to talk to now. (It's difficult to deceive a Cat!)

... and the child's a Rooster:
> The Cat never takes the Rooster seriously. It likes the fine feathers as little as the crowing.

... and the child's a Dog:
> Calm and peaceful Pussy makes the Dog very happy. Excellent if Mum is a Cat.

... and the child's a Pig:
> Perhaps – but the sentimental Pig suffers from the Cat's indifference.

*If the parent is a Dragon ...*

... and the child's a Rat:
> The Dragon asks a little too much of its children. But, one way or another, it all ends up working well enough.

... and the child's a Buffalo:

> The Buffalo does its best to satisfy the Dragon – but it's difficult. The Dragon likes a bit of a show, and the Buffalo, let's face it, is an introvert and a bit of a dull dog!

... and the child's a Tiger:

> Good. The Dragon enjoys a bit of prestige in the world of the Tiger – so the Tiger will listen to him.

... and the child's a Cat:

> The Dragon may be a little disappointed by the apparent lack of ambition in the Cat, but there will be no problems.

... and the child's a Dragon:

> Very good! Each will be proud of the other!

... and the child's a Snake:

> Yes. The Snake is wise to the Dragon and understands him – even though he's not going to be taken in himself!

... and the child's a Horse:

> Certain problems – but all's well that ends well.

... and the child's a Goat:

> Proud of junior's artistic nature, the Dragon will help the Goat a lot.

... and the child's a Monkey:

> Good relationship. The Dragon brings to the

Monkey its wisdom and experience if the Monkey needs any!

. . . and the child's a Rooster:
The Rooster obeys blindly, so the Dragon is happy! Very good!

. . . and the child's a Dog:
No – the Dog doesn't have for the Dragon the admiration that the latter considers to be his due.

. . . and the child's a Pig:
Yes. The Dragon can be useful to the Pig. doing everything in its power to assure Master P's success.

*If the parent is a Snake . . .*

. . . and the child's a Rat:
The Snake loves his family – and the Rat is far from displeasing him!

. . . and the child's a Buffalo:
Wisely, the Snake does all he can. But it's a hard life!

. . . and the child's a Tiger:
Problems here for the Snake: all that serpen-

tine intelligence is needed if we're going to find out how the Tiger ticks!

... and the child's a Cat:
Yes – but watch out! Mum's possessive, and Dad keeps to himself!

... and the child's a Dragon:
Yes. The Snake understands the Dragon.

... and the child's a Snake:
Which one ensnares the other? Better for the young Snake to get married as early as possible. Afterwards, it'll be too late!

... and the child's a Horse:
The Horse's independence poses problems for both sides!

... and the child's a Goat:
Fair enough, providing the family is comfortably off.

... and the child's a Monkey:
Huh! It's going to be 'Right, Monkey!' again – as it always is.

... and the child's a Rooster:
They understand each other very well. The Rooster is flattered to consider himself indispensable – even at the price of his own liberty.

... and the child's a Dog:
They're no earthly use to each other.

... and the child's a Pig:
> The Pig has to take great care not to find himself immobilized!

*If the parent is a Horse . . .*

... and the Child's a Rat:
> Catastrophic! Especially if the mother is a Horse. Storm in the family!

... and the child's a Buffalo:
> No! When mama and papa Horse insist on having their way, baby Buffalo never forgives them. He doesn't understand.

... and the child's a Tiger:
> Fair enough. The Horse leaves his little Tiger some independence and loves him too.

... and the child's a Cat:
> The Horse has other fish to fry – the kittens will be left in peace!

... and the child's a Dragon:
> Whatever happens, all will be well. Each will live his own life.

... and the child's a Snake:
> Baby Snake will judge his father or mother

severely – and put them in the wrong in case of conflict.

... and the child's a Horse:
   They understand each other so well that it could mean trouble: each counts on the other too much, perhaps.

... and the child's a Goat:
   Okay. The kid will be happy – but he won't get much help!

... and the child's a Monkey:
   Nobody could care less! No problems here, then.

... and the child's a Rooster:
   The baby chick will be disappointed and will find wanting his father or mother. And they'll just laugh at him.

... and the child's a Dog:
   The Dog finds it hard to understand egoism. But he doesn't need the Horse anyway.

... and the child's a Pig:
   Not the best. The piglet finds it hard to bear the egoism of the Horse, and the Horse understands nothing. But neither loses any sleep over it!

*If the parent is a Goat . . .*

. . . and the child's a Rat:
> What on earth can be done here? (If mama is the Goat the damage is less).

. . . and the child's a Buffalo:
> Worlds apart. They're no good to each other at all.

. . . and the child's a Tiger:
> There'll be no peace here! The Tiger risks devouring the Goat . . . heedlessly.

. . . and the child's a Cat:
> Yes – apart from the fact that the kitten cannot rely on the Goat.

. . . and the child's a Dragon:
> A lovely picture! If the mother is a Goat and the Dragon a son, it's perfect.

. . . and the child's a Snake:
> The Goat allows herself, willingly, to be monopolized by her child – on condition that he reciprocates.

. . . and the child's a Horse:
> Yes, as long as the Goat doesn't count on the Horse too much to look after her in her declining years!

... and the child's a Goat:
> Could be amusing – if unconstructive. When the two signs are mother and daughter, there will be a terrific 'togetherness'.

... and the child's a Monkey:
> Bizarre! Parents like this could amuse the Monkey!

... and the child's a Rooster:
> Mutual exasperation! There's no common ground here at all.

... and the child's a Dog:
> The Dog will take his distance very early – but he'll never let the Goat down.

... and the child's a Pig:
> Hah! Finally, it's the piglet who comes to the Goat's rescue. He loves her!

*If the parent is a Monkey ...*

... and the child's a Rat:
> This works. The Monkey can do what he likes with the children.

... and the child's a Buffalo:
> The Monkey always has a bit of glamour in

comparison with the Buffalo – and he knows how to capitalize on it.

... and the child's a Tiger:
Not so bad, really. The Monkey's cunning balances the strength of the Tiger. They'll work it out between them.

... and the child's a Cat:
Great! This is a bit of good luck for the Cat!

... and the child's a Dragon:
This is good, too. The Monkey can give a lot to a Dragon who's too confident and a little precocious.

... and the child's a Snake:
Not too bad – guile and wisdom can make perfect bedfellows.

... and the child's a Horse:
Hm'n ... Horse junior – although he's clever enough – mistrusts the cunning to which, perhaps, he'll fall a victim.

... and the child's a Goat:
Better make the best of this, for our she-devil is devilishly devoted!

... and the child's a Monkey:
Perfect accomplices! Mischief becomes mischief-and-a-half!

... and the child's a Rooster:
> The Monkey, subtly, pokes fun at the Rooster. The bird does what he can to please – but he's going to get hurt.

... and the child's a Dog:
> Difficult ... the Monkey finds that his off-spring takes life far too seriously – and from this springs teasing that the Dog cannot stand.

... and the child's a Pig:
> Excellent. The Monkey is very fond of his piglet. He'll teach him to be less gullible.

*If the parent is a Rooster ...*

... and the child's a Rat:
> Little arguments. Bickering. Nothing serious – but nothing warm either.

... and the child's a Buffalo:
> Yes. Despite an occasional peck at random, the Rooster will allow himself to be led up the garden path.

... and the child's a Tiger:
> The Rooster will be systematically opposed.

... and the child's a Cat:
> The Cat will let the cock crow – but follow his own inclinations!

... and the child's a Dragon:
> Agreement possible. The Rooster admires his baby Dragon a little too much – and that can mean trouble.

... and the child's a Snake:
> They'll talk a lot – but the laziness they share may be increased.

... and the child's a Horse:
> The Horse will never submit to the Rooster's authority ... and the Rooster won't know what to do about it.

... and the child's a Goat:
> The Rooster will have the impression of having hatched a duck!

... and the child's a Monkey:
> The Rooster will be beaten on all sides – but quite happy about it.

... and the child's a Rooster:
> A cock-fight! To be avoided at all costs under the same roof!

... and the child's a Dog:
> The Rooster won't know where he is. A dialogue of deaf men!

... and the child's a Pig:
>    The Pig is patient – but he'll act according to
>    his lights. And don't let the Rooster think he's
>    leading him by the snout!

## If the parent is a Dog . . .

... and the child's a Rat:
>    Despite his sense of duty and good-will, the
>    Dog is not too keen on the Rat.

... and the child's a Buffalo:
>    No. Complete and total incomprehension on
>    both sides! They judge one another – and find
>    each other wanting.

... and the child's a Tiger:
>    Good. The Dog will give a lot to his child, of
>    whom he will be very proud.

... and the child's a Cat:
>    They get on famously together – especially
>    papa Dog and Cat daughter.

... and the child's a Dragon:
>    These two do not get on at all. The Dragon
>    cannot bear the criticisms which the Dog, with
>    his clear mind, continuously aims at him.

... and the child's a Snake:

For the Dog, this is almost as though he had unwittingly flushed a viper! He's not fond of the contemplative kind of intelligence.

... and the child's a Horse:

It's not just that the Horse wants his own way – it's his selfishness that worries and disappoints the Dog.

... and the child's a Goat:

Difficult. Discouraged, the Dog may end up by washing his hands of the Goat.

... and the child's a Monkey:

The Dog won't take the Monkey seriously – and it's mutual!

... and the child's a Rooster:

They avoid one another. They have nothing in common. The Dog is irritated by the fine feathers the Rooster insists on wearing.

... and the child's a Dog:

A great togetherness here. It's a little dangerous for the rest of the family, though: they might carry it too far!

... and the child's a Pig:

Yes, although the cruder side of the Pig puts the Dog's back up.

*If the parent is a Pig . . .*

. . . and the child's a Rat:
Fine. They'll have a lot of laughs together – and if the Rat does take advantage a bit, who cares?

. . . and the child's a Buffalo:
Perhaps, even though the Buffalo is a little reserved.

. . . and the child's a Tiger:
Yes. But the Tiger will remain unsatisfied: he's always expecting something more.

. . . and the child's a Cat:
Very good, but the Pig will be upset by the Cat's unusual indifference towards family things.

. . . and the child's a Dragon:
Good. The Pig can even be useful to the Dragon.

. . and the child's a Snake:
This will work – at the Pig's expense. A mother Pig can become a complete slave to a Snake child.

. . . and the child's a Horse:
The inevitable departure from home of the Horse will upset the Pig – especially as it's always earlier than expected.

... and the child's a Goat:

> Lucky Dog! The Goat will be helped all his life by the Pig. They love each other.

... and the child's a Monkey:

> Great! The Monkey is constantly surprising and amusing the Pig – whom he respects, surprisingly!

... and the child's a Rooster:

> Lucky Rooster! The Pig will do everything to understand him and make him happy.

... and the child's a Dog:

> They get on well. The Pig will always back up the Dog in his Causes, but he'll make himself unhappy quite often.

... and the child's a Pig:

> Yes. A pair of real friends. They'll take great pleasure in each other's company and often go out together.

*What kind of business relationship can there be between ...*

... Rat and Rat:

> Where is the working capital? This could end up at the moneylender's or in the bankruptcy courts!

... Rat and Buffalo:

>The Buffalo is no businessman – but he is in a sense the working capital: it's enough that he gives the orders!

... Rat and Tiger:

>Luckily for the Tiger, the Rat – although a profiteer – is honest. Otherwise the Tiger might regret it!

... Rat and Cat:

>The Cat's terrific in business, especially for the Rat.

... Rat and Dragon:

>A marvellous association, as long as it's the Dragon who's the boss.

... Rat and Snake:

>Interesting to watch from the outside!

... Rat and Horse:

>An impossible pairing! They don't like each other and will do anything they can to harm one another.

... Rat and Goat:

>The Goat can bring his artistic approach to the Rat – but does the Rat know how to make use of it!

... Rat and Monkey:

>Yes – but the Rat must curb his blind adulation of the Monkey.

... Rat and Rooster:
> Reckless! They make very bad business to-
> gether.

... Rat and Dog:
> The Dog, although he is a realist, is too
> idealistic for the mercenary Rat.

... Rat and Pig:
> The Rat will try to trick the Pig, to put one
> over on him – but the Pig is so lucky in money
> matters!

... Buffalo and Buffalo:
> They'd be better off buying a farm!

... Buffalo and Tiger:
> A disastrous association: the Buffalo would try
> to put the Tiger out of business!

... Buffalo and Cat:
> Poor Buffalo! The Cat will take advantage of
> his acumen. But the Cat had better watch out,
> just the same!

... Buffalo and Dragon:
> Who's going to be boss here? And the Buffalo
> will seem to everyone to be playing stooge to
> our Mister Big!

... Buffalo and Snake:
> They'd better not ...

... Buffalo and Horse:

If they must! They're such hard workers, and the Horse is as honest as the Buffalo (although much smarter).

... Buffalo and Goat:

Out of the question. They can do nothing for each other.

... Buffalo and Monkey:

No! The Buffalo would be all the more hurt because he's fond of the Monkey!

... Buffalo and Rooster:

Lots of work, little profit – and the Buffalo is unable to appreciate the Rooster's good points: he finds him lazy!

... Buffalo and Dog:

They haven't a single idea in common! How could it work?

... Buffalo and Pig:

The Pig could be very useful to the Buffalo, whom he esteems for his output.

... Tiger and Tiger:

Not advised. They would take too many risks and should be kept apart!

... Tiger and Cat:

Possible. The Cat can be useful to the Tiger, and they complement one another: one being cautious, the other bold.

... Tiger and Dragon:

A worthwhile association of two go-getters. The Dragon can shine for both.

... Tiger and Snake:

No. They could never agree.

... Tiger and Horse:

Yes. The relationship will be complicated, violent – but profitable.

... Tiger and Goat:

The Tiger will judge the Goat impartially and with tolerance. But the Goat will often lose his nerve face to face with the Tiger!

... Tiger and Monkey:

The Tiger must be careful of the Monkey's cunning, and the Monkey of the Tiger's strength.

... Tiger and Rooster:

Absolutely not! The Rooster isn't in the same class as the Tiger: he would soon be exhausted.

... Tiger and Dog:

They can do anything together ... except go into business!

... Tiger and Pig:

The Tiger is so generous – and he doesn't realize that he is, in fact, a constant danger to the Pig.

... Cat and Cat:

> A congress of lawyers, a party of professors!
> Open an antique shop. In fact yes, yes, and
> yes!

... Cat and Dragon:

> Yes. The Cat will let the Dragon make the
> decisions – but he will give a lot of good advice
> first.

... Cat and Snake:

> Yes. They will do good business (as long as they
> stop talking and work!).

... Cat and Horse:

> Good sport here! The Cat will be mischievous
> but the Horse is big enough to look after him-
> self. And what a social life!

... Cat and Goat:

> The Cat has taste and knows how to choose.
> He can make the Goat productive. A profitable
> association.

... Cat and Monkey:

> A pointless exercise. Each is big enough to look
> after himself against the other – but neither is a
> creator!

... Cat and Rooster:

> The Rooster had better be careful: the fact
> that the Cat wants to do business with him
> conceals something.

... Cat and Dog:

> The Cat will be useful to the Dog through his cleverness and objectivity; the Dog to the Cat through his loyalty and materialism.

... Cat and Pig:

> Yes. The Cat is smart and the Pig has unbelievable luck. They can make a lot of money together.

... Dragon and Dragon:

> Problems of prestige here. Not advised.

... Dragon and Snake:

> Possible – but if the Snake allows the Dragon to do all the work, there could be fireworks!

... Dragon and Horse:

> It could work all right over single deals – but never for a long time.

... Dragon and Goat:

> The Goat could make it in a big way in some artistic enterprise, associated with a Dragon director, producer, or impresario.

... Dragon and Monkey:

> Great! Craftiness allied to power can hardly fail. They must stick together!

... Dragon and Rooster:

> If the Dragon pulls the strings, the Rooster could make a great public showing.

... Dragon and Dog:

No. The Dog sees through the Dragon – and Dragons don't like that!

... Dragon and Pig:

A surefire success! Especially as the Pig is relatively modest.

... Snake and Snake:

All planning and no action will make the business totter.

... Snake and Horse:

This could work: the Snake will think; the Horse will work.

... Snake and Goat:

Maybe. The Snake has the know-how – but he's hopeless at running the show. And the Goat makes mistakes.

... Snake and Monkey:

Headaches for the Snake here: the Monkey is a real smart alec.

... Snake and Rooster:

Talk talk, talk ... this business could sink in a sea of words!

... Snake and Pig:

The Pig has no need of wisdom and the Snake risks harm to himself.

. . . Snake and Dog:

>Possible, of course – but hardly tempting.

. . . Horse and Horse:

>Each will pull the bedclothes to his own side
>of the bed – and only one blanket for two
>Horses!

. . . Horse and Goat:

>Yes. The Goat will unconsciously be running
>risks – but the Horse is clever.

. . . Horse and Monkey:

>The Horse knows his way around too much to
>do business with the Monkey.

. . . Horse and Rooster:

>Okay. But the Rooster mustn't rely too much
>on the Horse's good-will: the Horse will not
>tolerate his idleness.

. . . Horse and Dog:

>Why not? Just so long as they keep it to busi-
>ness and avoid social contact.

. . . Horse and Pig:

>No good as a business team, this pair. They
>have different ideas.

. . . Goat and Goat:

>An odd pair, this! Two tramps under a bridge
>perhaps . . . or a two-man confidence-trick
>team.

... Goat and Monkey:

The Goat has nothing to lose and the Monkey recognizes his talents enough to capitalize on them.

... Goat and Rooster:

No good. The Rooster finds the Goat exasperating and useless. He simply doesn't understand Goats.

... Goat and Dog:

No – the Dog is busy with more serious things. At least, he thinks so.

... Goat and Pig:

They will be useful to each other. And the Goat – even the Goat! – can help the Pig.

... Monkey and Monkey:

If they keep on playing I'm-smarter-than-you, there could be trouble ahead.

... Monkey and Rooster:

Poor Rooster! He's going to find himself plucked!

... Monkey and Dog:

Nothing for either side here. The Monkey is afraid of the Dog, who won't let him get away with anything.

... Monkey and Pig:

The Monkey has every reason to team up with

the Pig and he knows it. It'll be in his interest. But the Monkey will be generous (that's in his interest, too!).

... Rooster and Rooster:
This way to bankruptcy!

... Rooster and Dog:
No, no! They don't have a single idea in common. It would be a disaster.

... Rooster and Pig:
The Pig has no confidence in the Rooster as a businessman, so he'll hold back.

... Dog and Dog:
They are not really interested enough. They'd be ruined because they couldn't care less!

... Dog and Pig:
Yes, but the Pig won't get out of the affair scot-free, because the Dog is too generous. They'll bamboozle the others, though.

... Pig and Pig:
They could make a fortune together. Let them have a go, in any case, for luck will be with them!

*If the Rat is . . .*

. . . Capricorn:
A severe Rat. Difficult to trap.

. . . Aquarius:
Intellectual Rat. A writer of authority?

. . . Pisces:
Imaginative Rat. Can do everything – including make mistakes!

. . . Aries:
Cornered Rat! Lots of aggressiveness here.

. . . Taurus:
Rat the Charmer! (Something between Mickey Mouse and Ferdinand the Bull!)

. . . Gemini:
Super-Rat! Escapes all the traps!

. . . Cancer:
Dreamer Rat. His castles in the air can prove expensive.

. . . Leo:
Bizarre Rat. Contradicting himself, he should pay attention!

. . . Virgo:
Rat of the Laboratory. Will manage to find his way through the labyrinths of life.

... Libra:
Conciliatory Rat. Aggression very much toned
down.

... Scorpio:
Virulent Rat! Destroys anything in its way!

... Sagittarius:
Energetic Rat. Succeeds – even in making
economies!

## If the Buffalo is . . .

... Capricorn:
No joker he! He's not there to make fun.

... Aquarius:
Subtle Buffalo. The iron hoof in the velvet
glove.

... Pisces:
Frolicsome Buffalo. Watch out for a kick-back
from the starting handle!

... Aries:
Ambitious Buffalo. Beware the horns!

... Taurus:
Tender beef! But a Buffalo is a Buffalo.

... Gemini:

> A Buffalo who's not really serious? It makes for a splendid companion, though!

... Cancer:

> Buffalo diminished. Risks never seeing the fruit of his labours.

... Leo:

> Spoiling for a fight! But at least he can get out of the conventional rut!

... Virgo:

> Sawn-off Buffalo. Would do better to stick to gardening!

... Libra:

> Sociable Buffalo. Knows exactly what to do.

... Scorpio:

> Dangerous Buffalo – stubborn, violent, the bitter end!

... Sagittarius:

> Buffalo in balance. The most characteristic – if a little exaggerated.

*If the Tiger is . . .*

. . . Capricorn:
Thoughtful Tiger, and an avoider, therefore, of disasters!

. . . Aquarius:
Brainy Tiger. Finds a way to strike a balance between thought and action.

. . . Pisces:
Mad Tiger (just a little, anyway!). Great fun, but dangerous, especially to himself.

. . . Aries:
Jet-propelled Tiger! Could break the sound barrier – so watch out!

. , . Taurus:
Well-balanced Tiger (except for a slight tendency towards excess sensitivity).

. . . Gemini:
Tiger for madcap follies. Gets away with them, too!

. . . Cancer:
Fireside Tiger. Just a great big pussycat, really.

. . . Leo:
It's not because there's a Tiger in his tank that he should take himself for a Lion.

... Virgo:
: Practical Tiger. Gets what he wants.

... Libra:
: Tame Tiger. Good to work with.

... Scorpio:
: Complicated Tiger. Expect anything – you'll probably get it!

... Sagittarius:
: Just the right kind of Tiger. Can go far ... perhaps too far!

*If the Cat is ...*

... Capricorn:
: Nostalgi-cat. Can be the most unbending, the least sociable.

... Aquarius:
: Devoted Cat. A splendid best-friend. Ought to write.

... Pisces:
: Cat-cat-cat. Yes, thrice Cat. And so nice to be with among friends.

... Aries:
: Wild Cat. Claws rarely sheathed.

... Taurus:

What a nice puss! Stays purring by the fire. No claws.

... Gemini:

Alley-cat. An un-calm creature. A risk-taker.

... Cancer:

Lap-cat. Doesn't mind doing nothing. Nice – but a bit weak.

... Leo:

Tiger Cat. Calm enough at first sight, but the claws are always out!

... Virgo:

Wise Cat. Draws the chestnuts from the fire.

... Libra:

Cat who likes to flatter. A little melancholy, feminine or effeminate, full of charm, pleases the ladies!

... Scorpio:

Witch's Cat. Look out for sorcery and spells!

... Sagittarius:

Exceptional Cat – the best, the most balanced, of all.

*If the Dragon is . . .*

. . . Capricorn:
Discreet Dragon. Doesn't court attention much
(at least not for a Dragon!).

. . . Aquarius:
Lucid Dragon. Even capable of self-criticism.

. . . Pisces:
Super-Dragon! Great wisdom and great in-
spiration. Could and should go far.

. . . Aries:
Hyper-Dragon! Charges with eyes closed, sure
of winning.

. . . Taurus:
Marzipan Dragon. A nice legendary creature
for the family. Restful.

. . . Gemini:
Multicoloured Dragon. Flames gush from
every nostril!

. . . Cancer:
Dragon with head in the clouds. Actually lives
in those castles in the air.

. . . Leo:
Exaggerated Dragon. His excesses can only ex-
haust you.

... Virgo:

A precise Dragon. The only one that is not fabulous, make-believe (you would almost think you were dreaming!).

... Libra:

Reassuring Dragon. But don't believe what you see: appearances are deceptive!

... Scorpio:

Spiny Dragon. Stroke him and prick yourself.

... Sagittarius:

This one, you *can* count on: he's friendly and quiet for a Dragon.

*If the Snake is ...*

... Capricorn:

Philosophical Snake. Great intelligence – if a little abstract.

... Aquarius:

Esoteric Snake. A bit worrying, with all that intuition! Should do well in spiritualism or clairvoyance.

... Pisces:

Water Snake. Will have plenty of self-composure. Cool as a cucumber.

... Aries:

Python. Watch those coils! – And look out for the battering-ram.

... Taurus:

Adder. Will be faithful – but that charm is irresistible!

... Gemini:

The Snake that keeps on stirring. The most inconstant one of all.

... Cancer:

Sleepy Snake. Will hardly kill himself on the job. Shake well before using!

... Leo:

Energetic Snake (a rare breed, without doubt the most balanced).

... Virgo:

Rattlesnake. Loves theatrical props – and knows how to use them.

... Libra:

Snake too polite to be honest! Be careful not to fall into his clutches: you could be hypnotized.

... Scorpio:

Lascivious Viper. This is the one that's always trying to persuade you to take a bite of that apple.

... Sagittarius:
> Decided Snake. Should reach its goal – but not
> terribly attractive.

## *If the Horse is . . .*

... Capricorn:
> Responsible Horse. Most exceptional (there
> will be problems, of course).

... Aquarius:
> Racehorse. Let's hope he looks after his jockey!

... Pisces:
> Pensive Horse. Even though spirited, he con-
> tents himself too often – simply imagining
> what he *could* be doing.

... Aries:
> Horse-power! Violent, bad-tempered, fiery.
> But if only some of those ideas could be fol-
> lowed through!

... Taurus:
> Cab-horse. The least egotistical of Horses.
> Makes concessions.

... Gemini:
> Thoroughbred. Won't stay still. Never finishes
> anything he starts.

... Cancer:

>Wooden horse. Too sensitive. Keeps going round and round the merry-go-round. Will never live his life as he wants to.

... Leo:

>Centaur. Capable of anything. Thinks only of himself.

... Virgo:

>Draught-horse. Efficient but – alas! – unreliable. Practical nature could be the saving of him, though.

... Libra:

>Circus horse. Will dance all the time with plumes on his head – but behaves exactly the way he wants to.

... Scorpio:

>Wild horse. The most thrilling – and the most passionate!

... Sagittarius:

>Farm horse. Keeps right on to the end – of his own instability!

*If the Goat is . . .*

. . . Capricorn:
> Considered Goat. The best of the bunch. Can do anything – but keeps those illusions!

. . . Aquarius:
> Mysterious Goat! Distrust all that intelligence at the service of such whims!

. . . Pisces:
> Inspired Goat. Can succeed in any art – but awful to be with at times!

. . . Aries:
> Combative Goat. Stubborn and argumentative . . . keeps to its point at the risk of bringing harm to itself.

. . . Taurus:
> Charming Goat, but *charming*! Its idleness may lose it everything if kind friends don't take it in hand.

. . . Gemini:
> Goat with no silencer! A real whirlwind! Try not to be too annoyed!

. . . Cancer:
> Good-will Goat . . . what a nice little kid!

... Leo:

Proud Goat. Hard to understand, because contradictory. Worth persevering with.

... Virgo:

Goat to munch on. Just a snack-baa really!

... Libra:

Goat in triumph! Be on your guard, though: you'll be the one wearing the horns.

... Scorpio:

Passionate Goat. Gifted and very dangerous. Sharpened horns.

... Sagittarius:

A decided Goat. Will be able to make itself useful, and will have at least the appearance of good-will. Take advantage!

*If the Monkey is ...*

... Capricorn:

Scrupulous Monkey (but everything is relative, of course!).

... Aquarius:

Introspective Monkey. Keeps the cards well hidden.

... Pisces:
Inventive Monkey. Knows how to swim at the deep end.

... Aries:
A heavyweight. Beware the gorilla!

... Taurus:
A harmless one, this. Full of charm, inoffensive – well, almost!

... Gemini:
An effervescent Monkey. Makes bubbles – and squeaks!

... Cancer:
Nice little Monkey. Wouldn't harm you for a penny (try two!).

... Leo:
An eager beaver! He's caught a tiger by the tail!

... Virgo:
Manual Monkey. The least cerebral of the tribe.

... Libra:
Monkey-on-a-stick, or perhaps a tight-rope. Balancing all the time, he aims to please everyone – and risks falling off!

... Scorpio:
> Monkey without scruples. A big bag of tricks.

... Sagittarius:
> Monkey on look-out. Let him be!

*If the Rooster is ...*

... Capricorn.
> A rare bird. Profound qualities.

... Aquarius:
> Rooster on his dignity. An odd fellow!

... Pisces:
> Weather-cock. From his position on the steeple, aims high. Full of plans for castles in the air!

... Aries:
> Fighting cock. His aggression knows no bounds. Will pick a quarrel with anyone.

... Taurus:
> Cock in clover. Will be relatively easy to deal with.

... Gemini:
> Rowdy Rooster. Perpetual motion. Never stops!

... Cancer:
> Sincere bird. Will be plucked often!

... Leo:
> A tough one! Courageous cock who will give his life for anyone or anything.

... Virgo:
> Country cock. Both feet firmly on the ground.

... Libra:
> A tasty bird. Diplomatic, nice to know, conciliatory.

... Scorpio:
> Subtle Rooster. The most interesting. The pick of the bunch.

... Sagittarius:
> Cock of the walk. Larger than life.

*If the Dog is ...*

... Capricorn:
> Watchdog. You can count on him – but he is nervous.

... Aquarius:
> Wise Dog. The intellectual of the pack.

... Pisces:
> Four-footed friend. Interested to learn how to swim.

... Aries:
> Dog-of-war. Launches himself into the un-
> known.

... Taurus:
> Faithful Fido. Less cynical – and less lucid –
> than the others.

... Gemini:
> Mongrel. Bad head; good heart.

... Cancer:
> Dog-you-can-get-at. Sensitive, vulnerable,
> honest, violent. Will always sacrifice himself
> for others.

... Leo:
> Noisy Dog. Barks a lot to keep the enemy from
> the gates.

... Virgo:
> Technical Dog. Will not draw a bow at a
> venture.

... Libra:
> Doggie-dog. Rather a feeble creature. Needs
> to use tact and persuasiveness.

... Scorpio:
> Dirty Dog. Mistrust his eagerness to fight.

... Sagittarius:
> Prancing puppy. Nothing stops him!

*If the Pig is . . .*

. . . Capricorn:
A Pig who is austere . . . for a Pig!

. . . Aquarius:
Efficient Pig. Balanced. He'll make it.

. . . Pisces:
Inspired Pig. Perfection. A real swine!

. . . Aries:
A kind heart in a Pig's head!

. . . Taurus:
Piglet in a poke – but absolutely charming!

. . . Gemini:
Zany Pig. Will go far if the little pigs don't gobble him up.

. . . Cancer:
Gingerbread Pig. He must be careful not to be eaten.

. . . Leo:
High-class Pig. Guaranteed pure pork.

. . . Virgo:
Piggy-bank. Always right on the beam.

... Libra:
   Twice a Pig! The king of the mugs! Will end
   up spread on toast!


... Scorpio:
   Tough ... for a porker! Can play some dirty
   tricks nevertheless.


... Sagittarius:
   A logical kind of a swine. Always asking himself if it's ham or bacon.